Recognizing Unhealthy Relationships

Guide to Healthy Love & Self Discovery

Edited By Jennifer Jovanovich
Published November 2005 in Atlanta, GA, USA
Copyright 2007 Hauslendale Publishing
ISBN # 978-0-6151-4904-2

Table of Contents

About the Author   7

Introduction   11

Exercise 1   23

Identifying the Pattern

Exercise 2   47

Addressing Your Roles in Relationships

Exercise 3   61

Dealing with Your Issues

Exercise 4   81

Forgiveness

Exercise 5   89

Signs of Unhealthy Relationships

Exercise 6   113

Overcoming Fear & Anxiety

Exercise 7   123

To Stay or Go

Exercise 8   137

Signs of Healthy Relationships

Exercise 9   145

Awareness

Exercise 10   155

Recovery

Exercise 11   167

Rebuilding Trust

Exercise 12   175

Trying Again

Exercise 13   185

Turn Darkness to Light

Exercise 14   193

Making New Habits

Exercise 15   203

Taking Care of Yourself

Exercise 16   215

On the Rebound

Exercise 17	225
Abandon Drama	
Exercise 18	231
Quality of Life Assessment	
Exercise 19	249
A Healthy Self Image	
Exercise 20	259
Growth Assessment	

Dedicated to my husband for showing me a different way of life, and to my son for teaching me about parenthood and childhood at the same time.

Special mention to P.S.Y. for inspiring me and reminding me of my own ventures. May the unexpected come your way, but may it be healthier this time.

About the Author

Author Meilena Hauslendale began her career at a very young age working as a journalist, a freelance author, and contributor. In 1997, Meilena initially developed her style by displaying her art and inspirational sayings internationally through galleries and publications. It wasn't until 2002, that she began publishing her writing in the form of personal development articles and books.

"I always wrote in journals since I was a little girl. I wanted to capture my thoughts and feelings about the world and my surroundings. I wanted to write about all the lessons I was learning and the processes I had to go through in order to learn them. As I began writing, I would also expand my entries towards writing about others' lessons through my observation. The combination of the two allowed me to write from a generalized perspective, and therefore, allowed me to reach a broad audience."

The unique combination of art and literature had drawn recognition from both the art and writing community. In 2004, she was inducted into **Who's Who of American Women for 2004-2005,** the definitive biographical resource featuring the most accomplished women in all areas of human endeavor. Her first published book, Making Your Purpose Your Business, was released in March 2005, based on the series of articles used to guide people to seek and develop their purpose.

About two months later, Meilena began working on the book, Recognizing Unhealthy Relationships, inspired by her self-entitled article.

"Once I had released the article to Recognizing Unhealthy Relationships, the response was almost immediate. Several publication requests came in, and even readers started writing to us about the impact the article had on them and their family members. It was very gratifying to see the effect less than 1,000 words

could have on people. Not long after that, I began working diligently on the book."

Introduction

One of the reasons why I wrote this book is because I think we all at one point or another tend to realize that we are complex in the sense of our being. Because of this, the relationships we enter are complex. There is a lot going on when two people come together and combine their lives and experiences. Sometimes two people can work together and combine their lives interchangeably. And sometimes two people are just not compatible with their lifestyles or goals.

As long as there are people walking this earth, there will be relationships. There is no way around it. You will always be faced with the challenge of having some type of human interaction. Whether you have love relationships or friendships, they are still a combination of two people communicating together. And because no one person is alike, we do tend to experience the beauty of relationships, the combination of likes and dislikes.

The world would be a very boring world if we were all composed of the same programming. We need differences as they allow us to grow and change. They allow us to see a different side of ourselves that we might have not seen before. Relationships can bring out the best in us. They can also bring out the worst. Regardless of what type of relationship we endure, we are able to take the experience with us. We are able to walk away with the knowledge of knowing what it was like to work with someone different from ourselves. We are able to expand our ability to love.

Some relationships are healthy and some are unhealthy. We learn the difference between the two when we start interacting with others. Relationships may bare similar characteristics, but they will always be different in many aspects, as no one person is exactly alike. You could read about relationships all you wanted, but you won't know until you actually go out there and have one, what is healthy and what is not.

What works for one couple does not work for all. Everyone has different ideas of what makes up a healthy relationship and what makes up an unhealthy one. This book provides some guidelines to allow you to distinguish for yourself what is right or wrong for you.

When we look at how complex relationships are in general we have to break it down into parts to really dissect trouble areas. When you have two people coming from two separate backgrounds, you also have two pasts. Anything not dealt with in the past remains an issue to the individual. Whatever issues remain are then taken into the relationship as a whole, whether the partners realize it or not.

One of our focal points here is to assess your role in relationships such as family, friends, and love relationships, then take a look at any patterns that may have developed over the years. Once we bring our life patterns into awareness, we are able to identify unhealthy behaviors and work towards improving our daily relationships.

Once we have dealt with our issues or at least made progress to bring them into the forefront, we can then see our relationships for what they are. It's about being honest with yourself and your partners. You may have a healthy relationship but have unhealthy behaviors. Or it may be the other way around, and you may have an unhealthy partner that enabled your unhealthy behaviors.

This book allows you to place the focus on yourself and your involvement. By doing this you are then able to realize and hopefully see how much control and power over your relationships that you really have. You do have the power to choose. It is just a matter of becoming aware of that choice.

This book allows you to sit back and read, but it also asks of you to do some work. You will be challenged to perform introspective exercises after each chapter. These exercises will help you realize your behaviors and the behaviors of those around you. One of the best ways to achieve a healthy perspective and relationship is to make time to realize all the aspects of yourself that work for you and against you. The exercises will allow you to organize your thoughts in a therapeutic order, each step aids the other. You will get whatever you put into the exercises. If you work diligently at your self exploration, you can expect to achieve great results. So take time to answer some of the questions proposed to you.

In order to get started with your reading, you will need two standard tools. First, you will need patience. It's imperative that you practice tolerance with yourself while you go through this process of purging the old to let in the new. Each step you take will have its own time schedule. Accept your discoveries as they are. Accept the answers as they come to you. Some may come to you quickly and others will take time. Go at your own pace and you will get the answers you need at the time you need them.

Secondly, you will need a designated journal in order to benefit fully from this book. Each chapter will have a series of questions for you to answer in your journal. The questions are designed to get you to bring your life into focus and awareness. Each entry will allow you to reflect on different areas of your life that may have been overlooked or neglected.

Once we start to uncover different areas in our lives, we are then able to see ourselves for all the parts that make us who we are. This emotional purging allows us to create more room for loving relationships. This book is designed to help you take control over the choices you make in your life. You have the power to start over. You have the power to learn new ways of living. And you do have the ability to choose healthier relationships by becoming aware of what healthy relationships actually are.

It is my hope that this book will find the right people at the right time in their lives. So if you stumble upon this book it is not by accident. This book is intended to spark your awareness of your involvement in relationships and the type of people you have chose to surround yourself with.

All the answers you need are within your grasp. You just have to ask the right questions to trigger your memory. This is not a lazy man or woman's book. This book requires effort, *your* effort. It is up to you to read each chapter carefully and make an attempt to complete the journal entries.

If you have never kept a journal, don't be intimidated by starting one. Keeping a journal is a healthy way of getting your emotions out. It is also a great way to keep track of some important events that you may want to refer back to. Journals help you evaluate some of your actions and choices that you have made in life by placing them right before you.

Not only do I want to help you recognize some of your unhealthy relationships, but also some of the unhealthy behaviors within yourself that contributed to them. Relationships are not one sided, so when something is unhealthy, there are often two people that are held accountable. Granted you are not responsible for another person's actions, but you are responsible for your actions and reactions.

This book will help you not only identify unhealthy relationships, but also help you seek a way out, and put and end to the pattern. Your main challenge is to regain the focus on yourself so that you can have the strength to make a change.

It takes a lot of courage to make healthy changes for yourself, especially if you have lived that way for so long. There are people out there that have lived in the same unhealthy relationship for years, even decades. No case or instance is hopeless, no matter what your age. You are entitled to live a happy life. You owe it to yourself to seek this happiness and to seek this health.

Unhealthy relationships can really baffle us and leave us struggling to reclaim our sense of self. Know that no situation is permanent. There is a way out. You just have to be willing to take the steps necessary to re-train your own behaviors and choices.

Each chapter will help you identify your involvement and some of the key characteristics of emotional and physical abusive relationships. If at any time you feel highly mentally unstable due to severe emotional or physical abuse, please seek counsel. If you feel that you are in any type of danger, either to yourself or by the partner you are involved with, refer to your local community pages in your phone book to contact an abuse hotline or support group.

Nobody will think of you as a failure for going and seeking help. If they do, then you need to re-evaluate their importance to you. You are your own responsibility. So it is up to you to recognize when you are feeling weak and need to seek support for strength. You will still have to do the personal development work to repair yourself, but it helps just knowing that support is there when you need it.

If you feel like your life or the lives of your family are being threatened by the partner you are with, seek shelter. Get your family or yourself to safety as quickly as possible. Call a friend or family member and see if there is a safe place you can stay until you can support yourself. Use common sense here and don't wait any longer. You can figure out your involvement and the roles of your partner after you are in a secure place to do so. Dealing with your issues and reasoning will come later, but safety has to come first.

This book isn't merely about pinpointing character defects in your partner or previous relationships. Granted, we will discuss several characteristics that make up an unhealthy relationship and partner, but you will be asked to focus on yourself and your role in the relationship.

Your challenge is to unite your past and present so that you are able to see how your experiences interact with one another. There is a direct correlation between the two. However, we can not always identify them easily. Instead, our past issues might be buried one on top of the other. The longer the issues fester, the more they snowball and collide into our present day life and relationships.

What happens is that your judgment may become impaired and your choices clouded. You may have trouble distinguishing between healthy choices and unhealthy choices. The distance of right and wrong might not be far in between.

It is my sincere hope that you will be reminded of your intuition and your ability to make healthy choices in your life. Even if all the information in this book does not pertain to your particular situation, at least you can use it to create your own personal dialogue.

It is when we stop to listen to ourselves that we hear the most. May there be much light that comes your way.

Exercise 1

Identifying the Pattern

At the core of every relationship, there are two people that enter into a mutual partnership, both with two separate backgrounds. This creates a beautiful diversity; one where each person can benefit from the differences each one has to offer. However, differences can create conflicts, especially if there are underlying issues that each party is dealing with.

When we enter into companionships, we take everything with us. We take our securities and our insecurities. We take our strengths along with our weaknesses. We take our present day life along with our past. Any issues left unresolved become packed suitcases along our sides.

All these factors determine how we live our life and how we choose our relationships. For example, if you have had issues with alcoholism or drug addictions in your family history, you may actually seek a relationship that mimics your previous role. On the other hand, you may actually take on the addictive behavior yourself. Or if you had an emotionally or physically abusive family history, you may choose to be with a partner that shows the same characteristics.

We don't realize how much power we have over the choices that we make in our life. This is because we have not addressed unhealthy patterns that were established in our past. Just removing ourselves from unhealthy family histories does not rid us of the problem. In fact, as we enter adulthood, we encounter even more choices, and even more demands on the type of relationships we choose to engage ourselves in.

The pattern lives on, until we are willing to recognize the corrections we need to make with our own behaviors. You can blame your partner for being the root of the problem, but the reality of it all, is that you chose to be with them. For whatever reason, you felt comfortable with that person, whether their behavior was healthy or not.

Part of being human is that we have free will. Along with that free will, we have the power of choice. Our choices are affected by what our experiences are in life. If you have had a perfect life, perhaps now you seek relationships with imperfections. If you have had a life of imperfections, you probably have sought relationships that either imitate your previous role or dominate your previous role. There are a variety of different scenarios that can represent life patterns. Patterns are unique to the person that creates them. Either way, these patterns will continue on, until you have addressed your own actions and the actions of others.

Sometimes in order to go forward, we have to accept taking a few steps back. We have to look for the root of the problem and see where some of our behaviors stem. We have to retrace our steps and our life events to gain a better understanding of who we are, and the relationships we surround ourselves with.

Patterns repeat themselves despite their counterparts. We may enter one unhealthy relationship and leave, only to find another in its place. The names may change. The people may change, but the same unhealthy behaviors still exist. Some people may view this as merely a series of unfortunate events. However, there is a greater force at work here.

In fact, these series of difficult events can actually allow you to hit a bottom with your behaviors and others. Difficulty enounces that there is a change waiting to occur. The worse things become, the closer we are to getting out on the other side of the situation. That is of course, if you are listening to yourself, and paying attention to your instinct. Ignoring your intuition could prolong your situation.

If you ever ask someone in an abusive or emotionally draining relationship if they chose to be in their current situation, chances are they may not recognize their own participation. This is often caused by a lack of awareness. When you don't recognize your patterns in life, it is hard to recognize your patterns in relationships.

Situations do happen to us by chance, but then there are situations that we subconsciously seek. We might be attracted to situations that compliment our behaviors, whether they are healthy or not. Do not confuse subconscious relationships and attractions with violence. In the instance of violence and abuse, the victim's choice was taken away from them. In a relationship, both parties consent to being with one another.

First we need to realize that we contribute to our own personal well being. We contribute to what we become and the people we attract. Once we recognize and actually admit our participation in relationships, we can then realize that we contribute to the unhealthy behaviors present in the relationship.

Our reactions and actions are based on our previous 'practices' with relationships. Typically the first forms of relationships we encounter are with family. They create the foundation for us to grow. Some people come from very loving homes and they do not have to experience extensive emotional trauma or abuse. Others are not as fortunate and have to endure a different path, one that may have several unhealthy factors involved.

Although there are many people that overcome their family obstacles, they still have to deal with the after affects of any trauma they had to face. These scars can cause subconsciously unhealthy choices. You may not even realize what type of choices you are making with relationships. You may have not even recognized that your past experiences have contributed towards your personal makeup.

Part of the reason why we don't pay attention to certain circumstances or life events is because it is a coping method. When our minds and bodies undergo a certain amount of emotional or physical stress, they can react in several different ways. Some people isolate themselves. Some people may become severely depressed and turn un-dealt issues inward. Or they may deal with the issues in an outward fashion and relive their past by recreating the event, except just with a different stage.

Many people don't even acknowledge that the emotions existed. The awareness was there perhaps initially, but then after repeated occurrences immunity was established, and the awareness was then temporarily ignored. Without awareness, there is no growth. There is only repetition.

Ignoring our own awareness or intuition is a defense mechanism that allows us to try and temporarily cope with the situation we are in. However, this is only a temporary fix as your body can begin to yield different physical results verses only emotional.

Physical stress such as illness, anxiety, headaches, or just irritability can begin to set in when you have ignored the emotional warning signs. Your first indication that something is not right should actually be from your gut instinct or your intuition. Once you ignore your intuition, your body has to step in and send out a warning.

Unfortunately people adapt to this unhealthy way of life. They ignore their intuition instead of relying on it. This is easy to do if you have not identified the root of the cause. In order to begin having healthy relationships, we must first address our unhealthy ones.

Get a notebook and dedicate it to your personal evaluations of your relationships. Our first exercise we are going to focus on identifying all of our relationships from the past up till current. You don't have to write down every single relationship and friendship you ever had, but do write down the relationships that were proven to be significant to you.

At the end of this chapter you will see a sample guide on how to create your relationship assessment. You can either recreate this assessment sheet yourself in your notebook or you can copy it on a copier and enlarge it so you are able to write on it. You may need to print out a couple of sheets to be able and fit all of your relationship information. You don't want to leave anything out here. Be thorough with your assessment.

Write down the relationships that you have had that are both unhealthy and healthy. The only way you can fully assess your roles in relationships is if you see them all right in front of you. Take the time to neatly organize your relationships into a timeline. This will allow you to see how your relationships have developed with age. Mark somewhere on the side of your columns something to the effect of 'beginning' relationships and 'current.' Start out by recalling your earliest relationships and then your work your way toward your current ones.

Make an additional column for your personal notes. Give yourself plenty of space for the evaluation notes. You can use as many pages as you feel necessary. You want to be able to really identify the nature of your relationships in black and white.

Create one more column labeled 'my role' or whatever you wish to call it. This column will be used to identify what role you played in the relationship. Were you an enabler? Were you always trying to be in control? Or were you playing a victim? Maybe you were even the aggressor in the relationship. Whatever role that you felt you played, write it down.

Be honest with your answers. This exercise is intended to open up your awareness and help you recognize your involvement in the relationships you carry out. If you feel emotions while you are writing your evaluation, welcome them. Emotions are indications that you are opening up your senses and allowing yourself to feel.

When you allow yourself to feel, you are allowing yourself to look at your life as it really is. This can be an intimidating moment because you are revealing certain areas of your life that may have been covered for a long time. When we hide our feelings or block out our awareness, we let our emotions blister. So it would only be natural to experience some emotion along with the recollection.

Know that the emotional state you might enter will not last forever. Opening up your awareness may make you feel vulnerable, naked even. You are uncovering the dark areas of your life so that you are able to go forward into your own light. Not only will this evaluation help you with your relationship with yourself, but also your relationships with other people.

When you remove some of the darkness from your life you are able to create more room for loving healthy relationships. You might hurt right now as you uncover some of the dirt, but know that it will be worth it in the end. You are working towards your own sanity and definition of love.

Your first relationship assessment should start out with your family or guardian. Identify all the people that were closely involved with you. Think about what types of bonds you had with these people. Or what types of bonds you did not have. Did you feel complete or was there something missing? Most important, did you feel loved? How was love shown to you? How did you reciprocate this affection?

There are so many different characteristics that may have been shown or not shown to you. Write them all down as each one is an intricate part of who you are today. Don't censor your thoughts or emotions. Just allow yourself to look at your life as it truly is. There will be dark areas and there will be light areas. What matters is that we are taking the time to give each area of our lives the proper assessment that it needs. We are smoothing out the surface and perfecting an already perfect relationship with ourselves.

While you are identifying key relationships in your life, get in to both sides of the partnership, both your role and the role that others played with you. What we are analyzing here is the type of relationships we have established in our lives and the patterns that were made from them.

After writing about your family relationships, you can then expand to friendships and love relationships. What type of friends did you surround yourself with? What type of partners did you choose? Once you are done writing about all of your relationships up to this point in your life, go down your list and mark whether or not you thought the relationship was healthy or unhealthy. Be sure to keep this list as we will return to this list later on to assess it a second time.

Now go to the column that you had set aside to write about your role in the relationship. Be honest here and complete a role for every relationship you have listed. Even if you put down the role as being just 'daughter' or 'son,' expand your answer and write about what type of role you played as a 'daughter' or 'son.' Even children have significant roles in their families' lives so it is essential that we discuss them. After all, this is really where it all began, your youth.

Once you have completed the large task of writing down your assessments, take time to meditate on what you have just discovered about yourself and your relationships. Did you learn something new about yourself? Did you identify any trouble areas you were unaware of? What areas sparked emotions in you?

Now that you have taken some quiet time to reflect on the relationships you have and had, create a separate section in your notebook to write down your thoughts. Write about how you feel now with your current relationships. Are you happy or unhappy? How is your health and over all well-being? What areas would you like to improve on?

Then create another section in your notebook and call it 'patterns.' Go back to your relationship timeline that you created and review it once more. Do you see the pattern? Do you see certain relationships that imitate one another, but perhaps are in a different form? Write about the similarities. Do you notice that you took on similar roles within the relationship?

Make sure you date your entries so that when you go back to read them, you can see how much you have grown. It will be interesting to see if your perspectives of your past and current relationships coincide with your new found knowledge of yourself and of what is a healthy and unhealthy relationship.

If you are able to see your pattern right now then that is great, but if you do not see a pattern yet, that is ok too. Sometimes we don't realize that a relationship is unhealthy, but yet we harvest the signs of an unhealthy relationship. There are people that stay in long term marriages and are miserable, but never stop to address why.

When we prolong unhealthy relationships we prolong our own unhappiness and others as well. We do affect others whether intentionally or not. We carry the weight or stress we experience with us wherever we go, whether it is work or at home, it is there. It doesn't go away until we address our involvement and face our issues head on.

You may not have any past or current issues to deal with or you may have a lot to deal with and don't realize it. Awareness begins with you. It is never too late to address your personal issues and battles. The only consequence is a better understanding of your life and the people you choose to involve in it.

Take as much time as you need with this assessment. It's okay to stop in between and rest your mind. Be patient with yourself during this process and you will allow whatever needs to manifest to do so. You might be uncovering issues that took years to create and develop so taking a few days or weeks to write about them and evaluate them would be understandable.

Sample Relationship Assessment Sheet

DATE:	Circle One Beginning Current	
		Relationships
		Unhealthy
		Healthy
		Your Role
		Their Role
		Notes

You can recreate this chart in your notebook vertically so that you have enough room. Feel free to improvise to accommodate your own needs. If you are working with loose paper make sure that you put it along with your journal. You don't want to lose something you have probably spent a lot of time writing and pouring your heart into.

You more or likely will need several sheets of paper for your assessment. This is to be expected. The more you write, the more you can get out of your assessment. You may even have other memories recalled after you start writing. They may come to you a couple days after you begin the process.

This assessment is the start of a cleansing, spiritually, mentally, and physically. The emotions you feel during this time may feel out of balance, but that is okay. We don't start out being perfectly balanced. We start out falling off the edges and then slowly making our way toward the center.

Some words of advice to all that begin this process. Don't be afraid of what you discover. There might be a lot of thoughts and feelings that get stirred up during this assessment. No feelings or emotions are bad. They all have value and are important as to what they express. Feelings only go bad when we use them to harm others instead of using them to understand our own good.

You might be tempted at some point to stop the process. If you feel this way, take a break, but don't give up. Don't give up trying to figure yourself out. When we understand ourselves, we can understand others a lot better. This is a challenge. There is no doubt about that. You are being asked to recover your past and then judge how it has affected you and your future.

Know that you only have to work one exercise at a time. Don't get ahead of yourself and try to work the whole book overnight. Some exercises will emotionally drain you more than others. It all depends what you have to deal with when they reach the surface. Our past experiences have been stored in many fine crevices so you will be surprised what you see, what you will feel.

Don't judge your emotions when they surface. Don't think that some of your thoughts and feelings are not valuable. If you have that mind set or that low of a self esteem, get over it. Everything you have to deal with is important and essential to you as a whole. The only way to get through hurt, anger, or sadness, is to let it out. Let it all emerge one by one. This is a special time for honesty and truth. This is a time especially for you.

Exercise #1 Journal Entry Summary

1. Identify significant relationships you have had in your life from your past to current. Start with friends, friendships, and then work your way to love relationships. Keep in a chronological order by occurrence so you can see how your relationships with others developed.

2. Identify your role in the relationship

3. Identify the partner's role in the relationship

4. Note whether the relationship was healthy or unhealthy

5. Take notes on how you felt when you were in the relationship

6. Write descriptions for the relationships you listed. Think of what type of relationship you had with this

person. How did you feel loved? Or did you not feel loved? How did you convey love?

7. Was there something you felt that was missing from these relationships? If so, what? If you were unsure what was missing, please indicate that in your assessment.

8. Date your entries so you are aware of when you made this relationship assessment.

9. Meditate on what you just wrote. Pay attention to your feelings or any emotions that may have resurfaced. Write them down.

10. Evaluate your current relationships based on what you wrote, then ask yourself if you are happy or unhappy? Is your health good right now or is it suffering? How is your overall well-being and mental state currently?

11. Make a separate section titled 'Patterns.' Go back to your relationship timeline that you created and review it once more. Do you see the pattern? Do you see certain relationships that imitate one another, but perhaps are in a different form? Write about the similarities. Do you notice that you took on similar roles within the relationship?

Exercise 2

Addressing Your Roles In Relationships

After you have identified the patterns and roles through your previous assessment, ask yourself if these roles were healthy for both you and the other person. Did your role allow for growth for both you and your loved one or was it inhibiting? We don't realize that we can unintentionally harm someone that we love by trying to take on their responsibility.

In fact we may view our actions as being caring or loving, when in actuality we are preventing our loved one from their own growth. This is a common role of being an enabler. An enabler is basically a person who tries to keep the peace in the relationship simply by doing everything they can to cover up another's unhealthy behavior. Whatever it takes to keep the other person 'happy' the enabler will take on.

This is a very exhausting role because what is actually happening here is that one person is trying to be responsible for two. Some people refer to enabling as caretaking which is a very true term, as one is literally caring in a taking manner without realizing it. You might think that if you are being an enabler or caretaker that you are giving everything of yourself and how could that be 'taking' away from your loved ones. What occurs though when we do everything for someone is we are taking away our loved ones' right to grow.

Think about your own growth and experiences. You have probably learned through trial and error. Your learning would have never taken place if someone had performed the task for you. It is merely a necessary process that we endure to learn more about ourselves and the world around you.

An enabler is someone that usually chooses relationships that are in need of repair right from the beginning. An enabler has a subconscious need to fix and repair the wounded or people they think need their help. Now this perception may or may not be true, but in the eye of the enabler, the person needs help.

Classic relationships that attract enablers usually involve alcoholics, drug addicts, or physical and emotional abusers. These relationships are comparable to a parasite and host partnership because one feeds off the other. The enabler has the need to try and fix 'it' and the partner has the need to 'control' any situation outside of themselves.

This leads us to our next role, the 'controller.' The controller is a person who sometimes lacks self control with certain behaviors, or even substances. So instead of focusing on themselves and their own faults, they focus on trying to control others behaviors. The more focus they have on controlling others thoughts and actions, the further away they become from themselves which is what they want. Focusing on themselves would be too much for them as they would have to view their own faults and acknowledge their own lack of control in their life.

Some people refer to the controller as the 'manipulator' as they are often trying to control situations through subtle points of manipulation. Their partners may not even realize that they are being manipulated as the controller's work is subtle. The controller starts out with small forms of manipulation and then as time progresses, they develop into larger requests, ones that can leave their partner baffled if not recognized.

Controlling behaviors take on many different forms. Some forms of control may be jealousy, physical or emotional abuse. These behaviors are often addressed with the label of 'love,' but they are not. What is even more obtrusive is the controller may not even be aware of their own actions. They may be just mimicking the behavior they saw in their family or from some sort of other powerful influence. They are repeating their own pattern and unless it is identified to them, it will go unchanged.

For some controllers even if their issue is addressed by their partner or a health professional, they may still be oblivious to making necessary changes. Controlling to them, takes on the characteristics of any other addiction or obsession. They have to hit a bottom. Situations have to hit an extreme low point before they will acknowledge the pattern or even realize their behaviors. If they are lucky, they will reach a bottom. If they are not, they will continue to find partners that conform to their ideals.

Even enablers have to reach a similar bottom. They have to become fed up of being treated poorly or their health has to get bad before they will pay attention. If they are fortunate enough to recognize the warning signs, then they will be able to work toward a change. Some people are not so fortunate and undergo severe trauma simply because they do not have the courage to stand up for themselves and walk away.

It is as if you were sitting in a tub of water and screaming for someone to save you from drowning. When all you really have to do is, stand up. No one forces you to stay in the situation you are in. You stay in unhealthy relationships because you do not have the esteem to leave them. Or you don't recognize that the relationship is unhealthy.

Identifying what role you play or what your role your partner or previous partners played is essential to help you gain an understanding of how you function in a relationship. No one deserves to be unhappy with the person they are involved with. Relationships are given to us to add to our life's abundance, not subtract.

Sometimes relationships work and sometimes they don't. Know that every relationship contributes to who you are and how you view others. You may not find your true companion the first time around, but you will fall into the right arms eventually, both in love and friendship relationships.

There are various other roles that you may identify with in your evaluation. Roles are personal characters that we play or revert to while interacting with others. The 'enabler' and the 'controller' are two primary examples. You are by no means limited to identify with them in particular. Only you know how you act in a relationship. If you don't pay attention to your behavior then take a moment to do so.

Start out by writing down your actions in a relationship, feel free to use either a current or prior relationship as an example or your behavior. The more recent, the better, as this will give you an idea on where you are and what roles you seek right now.

Think about what actions you show someone you love. Examine your motives. Are you doing things that take away from the other person? Are you doing things to cover up for their mistakes? Are you alienating yourself from other loved ones outside of this relationship? Are you still maintaining your own responsibilities such as self care, child care, work, and housekeeping? Has this person become a part of your life or become your life?

Love relationships are certainly complicated enough, but then throw other factors into the mix and the complexity doubles. Factors such as alcohol or drug addictions can present a lot of issues. Other personal issues such as eating disorders, depression, or prior histories of abuse, can all play a part in unhealthy relationships. Mainly because a loved one's personal battle affects everyone around them. The problem is not isolated to the person that has the issue. Instead the issue involves all close to them and even innocent bystanders.

"Nearly 14 million American adults meet diagnostic criteria for alcohol use disorders according to the National Council on Alcoholism and Drug Dependence," (NCADD,2002). So as an example that is 14 million Americans, affecting each person they have a relationship with; their families, their children, and their workplace.

The number of people being treated for depression has also increased dramatically. According to an article issued by the Washington Post on December 4, 2004, the use of anti-depressants in the past decade has skyrocketed. Every one out of 10 American women are taking anti-depressants such as Paxil, Zoloft, and Prozac. In 2002, the number of anti-depressants and other psychiatric drugs issued to children has tripled since the 6% reported back in 1994-1996.

According to Britain's North Wales Department of Psychological Medicine estimates that as many as 30 million Americans take antidepressants. These statistics only further address the need for us to look at ourselves and our choices more closely. If we each took the time and responsibility to identify our issues and work towards their resolution, we would improve ourselves and the relationships around us. The impact even on one individual creates a powerful example for others.

Addressing our behaviors and dealing with our own issues may sound like a difficult process, and it can be an emotional adventure. However it is a very freeing process. When you actually look at your own actions, your own roles, you are able to understand why you do what you do. It is only until then that we are able to work towards correcting unhealthy behaviors and replacing them with healthy ones. We have to relearn love.

Not just the label 'love,' but the true meaning of what love is. For this exercise, go back to your timeline and take a look at your roles column. Do you still agree with what you have written? If your roles have changed since you have first analyzed them, just place a line through them (so it is still legible) and pencil in your new entry.

You may change your roles many times as your awareness and perceptions change. This is not a sign of indecision, it is a sign of growth. This means you are beginning to look at yourself as you truly are. These journal entries and notes are for you. Don't worry about their presentation, just focus on their function to you and your spiritual growth.

Make another entry in your notebook and be sure to date it. You should title your entry, "Addressing Your Roles in Relationships." Begin by writing about some of the roles you have played that have had an impact on you and your behavior. Write about your actions in those roles. Write about some of the emotions you feel when you think about those relationships. Write down what you think was healthy about your behaviors and then write down what you felt was unhealthy.

Make note on any similarities or traits that carried over from one role to the next. Maybe you felt more like a 'mother' or 'father' to a partner. Maybe you felt like a 'people-pleaser', always saying yes to whatever someone asked you to do even if it compromised yourself or other loved ones.

If you found someone that you truly feel you have found love with, your role will be as an 'equal.' You will feel as though you are on the same plane and despite any personal differences, you are always able to meet in the middle and experience harmony. You will not feel the need to dominate nor will you feel that you are inferior. You will feel that you are an important part of each other.

So although we are analyzing several different roles to help you recognize unhealthy relationships, it is important to also write about the relationships you felt were healthy. Both healthy and unhealthy relationships provide you with an opportunity to learn more about yourself. Give them both equal attention.

Exercise #2 Journal Entry Summary

1. Did your role allow for growth for both you and your loved one or was it inhibiting?

2. Did you take on someone else's responsibilities in the relationship?

3. Start out by writing down your actions in a relationship, feel free to use either a current or prior relationship as an example or your behavior.

4. Think about what actions you show someone you love. Examine your motives.

5. Are you doing things that take away from the other person?

6. Are you doing things to cover up for their mistakes?

7. Are you alienating yourself from other loved ones outside of this relationship?

8. Are you still maintaining your own responsibilities such as self care, child care, work, and housekeeping?

9. Has this person become a part of your life or become your life?

10. What role did you play in relationships you felt were healthy? Compare how you felt in a healthy relationship with your feelings in an unhealthy relationship.

Exercise 3

Dealing with Your Issues

Now that you have addressed your own role in your relationships, you need to identify the roles your partners played. This will allow you to see some of the unhealthy behaviors that may have existed on their side. Don't just identify behaviors found in love relationships, but also family and friends, any relationship where you feel someone else's behavior directly affected you.

You need to focus on the behaviors alone, not on blaming others for your own discontent. Separate the action from the person. When we separate the two, we are able to judge the actions as they truly are despite the person behind them. We can tend to look upon our loved ones with a kind eye, which potentially sets us up to allow unhealthy behaviors.

It is okay to be loving towards our partners, but that doesn't mean that we should tolerate unacceptable behavior from them. No matter how much love you have for someone it is not an excuse for mistreatment and abuse to occur towards you.

This exercise is intended to get you to see what type of people you have chosen to involve yourself with. By looking at your partner's behaviors, you will be able to see a pattern that developed, both in your life and theirs. Look at what behaviors they had that were unhealthy. Then look at your own behaviors and pinpoint what unhealthy behaviors you displayed in the relationship.

It may take you years from the time an unhealthy relationship occurred, to recognize the true nature of the relationship. For example, say that you had experienced a traumatic event during your childhood. It may have been sexual, physical, or emotional abuse. Maybe you acknowledged it at the time or told someone close to you. You may have dealt with the situation however you could for the moment, and at the age you were at that time, but that memory still remained.

Write down the behaviors of others that directly affected you. If there was any type of abuse performed, take note of the event in your journal. Then take time to write about how you dealt with the issue. Do you still have emotions about the past event? Is it something that still bothers you now? It's important that you recollect these grey areas in your life so that they are able to become more of a black and white. This will not only help you deal with the issues, but it will also bring them into light.

As we grow into adulthood we carry these events along with us. They may go unnoticed from time to time, but they resurface when triggered. The event may have affected the way you carry yourself or the way you treat others. You may have experienced underlying insecurities or low self esteem due to the events that occurred. Maybe you blame yourself for another's wrong doing.

Unhealthy relationships impact our ability to trust. They affect our ability to love. Some people deal with these feelings by turning on themselves. They involve themselves in habits that numb their emotions temporarily. This is not a permanent fix at all. In fact, the further away they get from the truth, the more these emotions fester.

The emotions can fester until the person reaches a bottom and finally releases the emotions from their chamber, or the person will continue to become even more self destructive. Self destructive behaviors can manifest and take on many different forms. They can present themselves as obsessive behaviors, eating disorders, substance abuse, overworking, or through the constant pursuit of unhealthy relationships.

All of these behaviors can occupy their time and focus, allowing them to cover up the festering emotions, however, this is not a healthy solution. Not only will the person carry their issues with them, they will create a whole new set of issues and impact everyone that they come in contact with.

Instead of turning inward, other people might shift their negativity outwards onto others. They may repeat the same action that actually disturbed them or traumatized them. For example, a person that was physically abused may start repeating the same behavior as they grow older. It is the only other way they can revisit the issue, but in an environment where they are in control.

Instead of taking control over their emotions, they concentrate on recreating the situation where they are the initiator. This can be applied to people who have been sexually abused, alcoholics, drug abusers, physical abusers, and even criminals.

If you can deal with your issues before these behaviors manifest just imagine the number of people who would be impacted in a positive manner. This is where it is your responsibility to seek help or to help yourself. Some people are able to independently explore their own emotions and past without outside intervention. These people must be characteristically strong enough to look at their own darkness, analyze their response and their actions, and then focus on recovering from their issues.

You are able to recover from your issues by seeing them for what they truly are. This is where you remove the sugar coat and look at the reality of the situation. If something was wrong, it was wrong. If something was right, then it was right. Don't feel guilty for admitting or acknowledging that something was wrong or right.

Sometimes we feel bad admitting someone we loved caused us harm. This is because we are trying to protect them. In actuality, we are prohibiting their growth. Just like children, adults too, need to be told when they have done something right or wrong. It is how we learn the difference between the two by learning about our own boundaries and the boundaries of others.

You have to view your life as you would the life of a close friend. For example, let's say you experienced physical abuse as a child or in your past, and you never took enough time to deal with your feelings. Your goal would be to confront yourself and recognize that it was not your fault. Recognize that you did not cause the problem and then forgive yourself.

Some people may take another approach and torment themselves by thinking they are the ones to blame. Some people spend years and years living with this shame, while the abuser usually has gone on with their lives. So if you view yourself as your own best friend, you would certainly never want to see someone torment themselves for so long. You would want to see them rise above their pain and turn into something useful.

Turning your past pain and issues into something that could benefit others and benefit your own well being is a path to healthy recovery. Rise above it instead of staying below it. Write down your issues and talk to a close friend that you trust. Tell them what you are doing and see if they would be willing to discuss or listen to some of your issues that you are trying to work with.

If you don't have a close friend that you feel confident enough to trust, then don't stop your progress or make it an excuse to stop looking at yourself. Go on. If you have to do this by yourself it is because you are supposed to and you spiritually have the strength to do so.

You have to have strength to deal with your own issues because it can be a very emotionally challenging adventure to endure by yourself. You have to be able to go back and allow yourself to feel the emotions you never allowed yourself or never knew that you could feel. This is part of your healing. You have to work through the pain in order to go forward otherwise it is only a roadblock in your life. Pain can be passed on to others without you even realizing it. Let the unhealthy pattern end with you.

If you feel at anytime that you need to seek outside help for recovering from trauma or to deal with personal issues, there are many different options made available to you at little or no cost.

If you are a high school or college student, counselors or psychologists are available for free typically. Contact your school office or student services department to set up an appointment. They will be able to help you out initially. If you feel you need long term one-on-one sessions then they should be able to refer you to other resources. If you are in a working environment, you can contact your human resource department to find out if they offer any employee counseling support.

There are other options such as self-help or support groups. Most support groups post their announcements in your local newspaper or classifieds. They are member supported groups which means that they usually survive on member donations. These meetings are almost always free and held in different facilities in your local city. Support groups are not counseling sessions. They are a group of people who have gone through or are going through a common issue.

You can just sit and listen or you can share your situation. Support groups can be great for people who have allowed their issue to isolate them. It helps to know that there are other people going through similar experiences such as you. It may also show you that there is hope for you to overcome your own obstacles. You may even meet some great friends too.

Whatever you need to do to address your own issues, do it. Personal battles will only hold you back in the long run and life is too short for that. It is up to you to take the initiative to look at yourself and your life with an honest eye and an honest heart. Making ourselves immune to these emotions not only temporarily blocks the hurt we feel, but also blocks the love we *could* feel. The space has to be there first. We have to make room for the good in our own hearts.

Support groups and counseling do not always work for all people, all the time. Some people require an individual approach. This book will provide a sample of how you can begin to work through your issues, however if you find a better way, that works for you, then feel free to develop your own method. Healing occurs and takes shapes in many ways, so embrace whatever method that grabs you.

One of the greatest ways to view your life is by writing it down. So return to your notebook and make a section titled, 'Issues,' or whatever you want to call it, just so you know what it is about when you want to return to it. This is reflective journaling because it creates a mirror on paper that you need to be able and see. It reflects who you are and how you feel at that given moment.

You might return to your journals and read over your previous entries to see your growth. Again, sign and date your entry, this is your own personal history you are creating. What we want to do is to link your past with your future and lay it out in front of you so that it all makes sense and you can see everything clearly. Don't restrict yourself or hold back anything while you are writing your issues down.

First start out by recollecting any situation in life that impacted you in a difficult way. Take a few moments to meditate on this before you do it and then when the urge strikes you begin writing it down. What you are doing is triggering your memory and your emotions. You will realize how powerful these memories are when you actually begin to release them. Write down how you felt at the time when your particular issue happened and then write about how you feel about the situation now?

What questions do you have unanswered? What emotions do you feel? Are you sad? Are you angry? Are you disappointed? Let it all out, but be in a safe place when you do it. Preferably, a place where you are able to be alone and reflect in solitude. If you need to cry, do it. If you need to speak out loud, then do it. Just make sure you write it all out. You need to explain to yourself the situation so you can work to resolve it.

So many people focus on the 'why me' question and the truth is that there is really no answer. Difficult situations happen to the best of people. Perhaps the situation occurred for a reason. It may be difficult to understand that reason while you are going through discomfort, but there is a greater force at work here. This may just be a part of your path. Training in life doesn't just come from schools, it also comes from life.

Once you have written all your main difficult issues down, you need to work on the resolution. You need to find some closure or peace of mind with yourself and the person involved.

You can find a resolution without even having that person there or without even coming in contact with them. The real person that has had to deal with the battle is you. That other person has their own issues, obviously, or they wouldn't have acted the way they had or treated you the way they did.

Now, if you are going over your issues and you had harmed someone else or may have acted wrongly towards someone, make a note of it, and where possible try to make an amends to the one you harmed. Sometimes, when we are living an unhealthy lifestyle we are completely unaware of its unhealthiness, because we have only had unhealthy lifestyles and relationships to compare them to. For some people, an unhealthy way of life is 'normal' and it takes a lot of relearning to gain a healthy way of life and future.

Dealing with difficult issues can go both ways. You have to look at who you may have harmed and the people who have harmed you. Sometimes we even need to go back and simply say thank you to the people that treated us properly or helped us through a trying time in our life. Maybe we didn't realize the value of their friendship or companionship at the time. Sometimes, when we are going through hard times, we don't always see the light shining through the window. So when we do sit down and review our issues with a clear eye, it is important to also remind ourselves of the good that occurred, however random or rare it may have been.

If you are unable to say thank you to that person's face for whatever reason, you can still express your gratitude by passing it on. I can almost guarantee that you will be presented with the opportunity to help someone else out in the future and it will be at the appropriate time when you both need it. Saying 'thank you' isn't always spoken in words, it can be carried out through actions.

After you have written all of your difficult issues out on paper, close your notebook, and put your pen or pencil down. Sit in a quiet place to reflect on all the emotions you felt. Pay special attention to each and every feeling that is coming to you. It is okay to take your time to recollect these issues and the emotions that surround them. Healing yourself takes time and practice.

You may need to mourn. You may need time. Or you may even need additional creative outlets. You might find that underneath your pain or discomfort, there are gifts. Maybe you will start painting, writing, or playing music. You may find some talent or hobby that frees you emotionally and physically.

Pent up emotions prevent us from being who we truly are. They prevent us from loving people the way we would really like to. They prevent us from sharing our life gifts with the world around us. They affect our self esteem and our perceptions.

When we release these emotions, we take back the power that they had over us and we put them in a more usable form. You can use your emotions as experience and motivators that stay with you for a lifetime.

As a summary, work on recognizing your issues by writing them down. You may not realize the emotions you have pent up until you write all the details down. Look at your involvement honestly and allow yourself to feel the emotions. Allow everything to come out as it should. Focus on your journal writing or any other creative outlet that you would like to use as a release, such as music, art, or even exercise.

Be mindful of self-destructive behaviors at this time. You are here to release your issues not create more of them. Be sure to give yourself plenty of rest and a lot of water. Take time to sit for 10-20 minutes in silence and meditate about this purification you are going through. Answers will come to you if you just listen.

Exercise #3 Journal Entry Summary

1. Address your partner's roles in the relationship. What are some of the behaviors they had?

2. What behaviors of your partner had an impact on you? What behaviors were directly affecting you?

3. How did you feel during this time? Did you have to go through any emotional, physical, or sexual abuse?

4. Have you ever been able to deal with those issues? If yes, how did you deal with your emotions? If no, how has your emotions from this event(s) affected your life?

5. Create a section called, 'Issues,' and begin recollecting any situation in life that impacted you in a difficult way.

6. Write down how you felt at the time when your particular issue happened and then write about how you feel about the situation now?

7. What questions do you have unanswered? What emotions do you feel? Are you sad? Are you angry? Are you disappointed? Let it all out, but be in a safe place when you do it.

8. Once you have written all your main difficult issues down, you need to work on the resolution. You need to find some closure or peace of mind with yourself and the person involved.

9. Make a list of the people we may have harmed either directly or indirectly, make amends to those people, either physically or spiritually.

10. Make a thank you list, of the people you would like to thank if you could, write down what you valued or learned about from them.

11. Write about any self-destructive behaviors that you perform. Ask yourself why you treat yourself this way. Then write down what you would like to change and make a plan to do it.

12. After you have written all your difficult issues out on paper, close your notebook, and put your pen or pencil down. Sit in a quiet place to reflect on all the emotions you felt. Pay attention to each and every feeling that is coming to you.

13. Be sure to give yourself plenty of rest and a lot of water. Take time to sit for 10-20 minutes in silence and meditate about this purification you are going through. Answers will come to you if you just listen.

Exercise 4

Forgiveness

When you start pouring your heart out onto the paper and looking at your issues, you realize that you have carried a burden for a great deal of time. The rest of the world seems to just go on with their lives and here you are with this weight on your shoulders.

The people that you may have had issues with or unhealthy relationships with have gone on with their lives, sometimes not even paying attention to how they may have harmed you. They may have stuffed their issues in the back of their minds, or worse yet, they have chosen to live unconsciously without paying attention to their involvement.

While you are allowing your emotions to resurface, you may seek a confrontation with these people. You may want answers or apologies. If the matter is criminal, you may have gained the strength to report the issue to the proper authorities. You will find a lot of ways that might help you gain closure and that is perfectly acceptable.

If you are involved in a relationship right now with the people that you have had the issues with, then a confrontation may be appropriate, especially if you wish to further the relationship. This may be the case with your family members. This is common with adults dealing with issues from their childhood. They may have not realized the strain they were under as a child, but as an adult they do.

You may want to acknowledge how you felt at that time and let the family member know what you were really going through. Sometimes they will respond and sometimes it will only lead to further disagreement. You have to be prepared for either one. When people live in denial for so long, they have a hard time accepting reality. They live in their own world, the one they created. So for any outside insight to appear, they may shun the thought and even blame you for acknowledging it.

You have to look at the person's current well-being health and put that into consideration. In some instances the person might have been unhealthy at the time they were involved with you, but have since then reached their own resolution. Or they could still be living an unhealthy lifestyle, and would not be able to identify with your confrontation because they are not able to identify their own reality.

When you initiate a confrontation with someone in regards to any issues you have had with them, it's best to think about what you are expecting to gain from it. Are you expecting them to admit they were wrong? Are you expecting them to change? Or do you just want to let them know how you felt and how the issue affected you?

Sometimes confrontations can really go over well and sometimes they can go over poorly. Not everyone will value your dealing with unresolved issues as much as you do, mainly because they don't have to carry your burden. Pay attention to the lifestyle they live currently, are they living a healthy lifestyle? If their lifestyle is unhealthy then don't expect them to give you something emotionally that they do not have or are ready to give.

You have to look at what you want right now. If the reason you are dealing with these issues is so that you can create a healthy lifestyle for yourself and your loved ones then your motives are true. If you are looking at your issues so that you can focus on changing someone else's lifestyles then you need to re-examine your role in that relationship.

The only person you have control over is you. We are focusing on your resolution and forgiveness with yourself. Forgiveness is about letting yourself know that you did the best that you could for the time that you had to do it. And with this principle we need to also apply this to our view with others.

Through forgiving ourselves, we can forgive those that harmed us or caused us discomfort. Forgiveness does not mean that we are allowing people to get away with what they have done. It does not mean that we are labeling what they have done to be wrong or right. It simply means that we are ready to acknowledge the wrong doing and rise above it.

Forgiveness is a process that takes time. Sometimes we can go back and forgive someone personally or sometimes we can simply forgive them in our hearts. Do what you feel is necessary. You may find that forgiving someone else is a lot easier than forgiving yourself.

Now that you have looked at your issues and your roles, you should know a little more about why you acted or reacted the way you did. You should have an understanding of what was really going on in your life. You should be able to pinpoint your feelings now. Look at what areas you felt were your fault. Look at what areas that you thought you were the cause, and also at the areas that you felt you were to blame.

Now take a look at the roles other people played in your situation. Did you see that they had something to do with the issue and that it wasn't just you? You were asked to write about others' roles in your life so that you could see in black and white, that there were more people involved besides just you. So looking at your results and assessments, how could you possibly place all the blame on yourself?

However, if you were at fault for the situation or if you were the one that had caused harm to someone else, you need to make amends for your actions. If you are able to do this directly to the person you had harmed that is great, but if you cannot due to the person being out of contact or no longer present, then you have to make some sort of spiritual amends either through prayer or meditation. Once you make your amends, then you can acknowledge your wrong doing and forgive yourself.

Make another section in your notebook marked 'Forgiveness' and write about the things you need to forgive yourself for. Maybe the resolution for you is working towards forgiving yourself and working towards changing the pattern or habit that caused you discomfort. Forgiveness is only half of the resolution, the other half is the action you to take to overcome your behavior.

Second, write down the people you would like to forgive and release, either contact them or make a spiritual act of forgiveness, whichever you feel is necessary. Remember forgiveness does not mean you are letting them get away with the wrong doing, it just means that you are acknowledging it as something you no longer need.

Your goal is to release a burden and to release emotions that have stood in your way. This moment is about rising above your situation. It is about taking hold of something greater and moving on to a higher ground. This is about owning your emotions instead of allowing your emotions to own you. You are embarking on a purification of mind and body.

Exercise #4 Journal Entry Summary

1. Make another section in your notebook marked 'Forgiveness' and write about the things you need to forgive yourself for.

2. Second, write down the people you would like to forgive and release, either contact them or make a spiritual act of forgiveness, whichever you feel is necessary.

Exercise 5

Signs of Unhealthy Relationships

Some of us don't even recognize that we are entering into an unhealthy relationship until we are so wrapped up into it we feel trapped. Then we may feel that we have time invested in the relationship and we should try to wait for a change. The unfortunate thing is that unhealthy behaviors don't change themselves. As a result, you may find yourself trying to fix something that has been broken for years, and is not in your power to fix in the first place.

The longer you wait to make a change, the harder it is to make one. The more time invested in an unhealthy relationship, the more difficult it is to leave. Let's face it, any type of relationship that you put time into is difficult to leave. There are even people that find it hard to leave jobs because they have so much time put in. Work environments provide us with relationships too. But you have to think of your well-being. Would you stay in a dead end job simply because of your relationships with co-workers? Or would go out and find something more compatible with your personal and financial needs?

Personal relationships are the same way. You wouldn't want to stay in an unhealthy relationship just for the sake of the other person, as you would really be doing them no good at all. Your unhappiness would begin to show and it would eventually affect your actions towards this person. We were not intended to live with others or be with others simply for the sake of pity alone. We were intended to find loving relationships with ourselves and the ones we choose to spend our lives with.

You want to make the most of your time and the most of the time you spend with others worth while. Investing time into a relationship that does not live up to your expectations, or a relationship that does not bare fruit, may not be something you want to stick with. Relationships are like puzzles, sometimes they fit and sometimes they don't. If the pieces don't fit, then don't force it. The key is to recognize the type of relationship you are pursuing.

A lot of times, when people enter unhealthy relationships, they don't even notice the choices they are making. Perhaps the main issue is they don't even know what normal is. This is very common among people coming out of corrupted families with unhealthy behavior. It makes perfect sense if you think about it. If you have never experienced a healthy relationship then you can only compare your current relationships with previous unhealthy ones. If you don't know what a healthy relationship is then it is kind of hard to try and pursue one.

This is where your previous evaluations can help you address the patterns that you are attracted to repeating. This is your first step at recognizing an unhealthy relationship. You need to address your own personal conflicts and repeat patterns. What issues keep reappearing in your life? Do you keep entering relationships where you are trying to 'fix' or 'repair' someone? Do you keep choosing relationships where the relationship is one-sided?

Unhealthy relationships and behaviors can be disguised in many different ways making it difficult for you to decipher what is healthy and what is not healthy. If you came from a family where everyone was involved in either obsessive eating, alcohol or drug consumption, or physical abuse, you might think that the behavior is normal and therefore healthy. If you came from a family that was heavily involved with criminal or gang activity, you might think that those behaviors are normal too.

That was one of the main reasons why when we first started our personal evaluation, you were asked to look at your relationships with family. You have to look at where you are coming from and understand why your perspective might be tainted from the very start. If your foundation of what relationships are suppose to be is distorted then you can usually expect your other relationships to be distorted as well.

Somewhere along the lines of our lives we have to teach ourselves or learn what healthy relationships are. Truth is sometimes we have to get sick before we can get better. We have to usually have something trigger our desire for wellness. We have to reach bottom. Everyone has their meltdown point, the point when they decide that enough is enough. They may not know what wellness is, but they are willing to commit to find a better way of life.

This desire is the most powerful motivator that you can have. Consider yourself lucky if you actually hit a bottom with an unhealthy relationship, it really can be a life changing moment even though it may seem like one of your darkest periods.

You have to want something better, even if you don't know what 'better' is. You might have an unhealthy relationship trigger this desire or you might even have some other life changing event take place. Maybe your health has triggered something. Maybe a book or a story triggered your senses. Whatever it is that reminds you that there must be some better way of living out there, use it as your wings.

When you invoke your curiosity about a healthier way of life, and the relationships involved with you, you are essentially researching what is healthy and what is unhealthy. Truth is, books can give you guidelines to help you identify unhealthy patterns and behaviors, but they can not tell you how to feel nor can they replace your own instinct.

That being said, we are going to identify some examples of unhealthy behaviors. Keep in mind that although you may see similarities in these examples, your situation is a personal one and should be treated as such. If you are in any direct or indirect physical harm in a current relationship, you should seek the proper authorities immediately and find a safe place where you can address your own involvement.

Your first priority is to protect yourself and any children involved. If you feel you are in danger, then your children are being exposed to that danger also, and you need to seek safety. It is one thing when unhealthy relationships affect us personally, but it is detrimental when unhealthy relationships affect innocent bystanders such as children. No relationship is worth compromising your children's well-being or livelihood. Remember, you are creating their foundation for relationships here, so pay attention to your actions.

If you are not in any physical danger, then you have time to assess your current situation or previous relationship choices. First understand that just because you are looking at your choices does not mean that any rash decisions have to be made. Once you identify unhealthy behaviors you can then work toward a solution. You will get all the answers you need at the exact time you need them, have faith in that.

Work towards discovering the cause for your choices, not the cause of the behaviors of the person you are with. Remember, if things are suppose to work out then they will regardless of the obstacles you face together. If the relationship is not supposed to work, then it will continue to experience challenges yielding little or no results.

Leaving the problem or the relationship is not always the cure. You either will continue the same pattern with a different face, or just return to the old one. Look for the root of the choice inside yourself. Be open to looking at your current or previous relationships for what they truly are. Turn the lights on.

Most people who are accustomed to unhealthy relationships stay in similar relationships because the behavior becomes comfortable to them. In fact, if they were to actually have a healthy relationship introduced to them, it would feel quite odd at first. For someone that is not use to being treated well, a healthy relationship may take time to get accustomed to.

This is because healthy and unhealthy relationships are very different in the emotions that they trigger in us. Healthy relationships allow us to experience a duality of companionship, meaning there are two people working together towards fulfillment, both in the relationship and in themselves. Unhealthy relationships occur when two people do not work together, or are incompatible with their desires to fulfill a commitment to one another.

Healthy relationships bring out the best of who we are. Unhealthy relationships can bring out the worst in us. You can often determine what type of relationship you are in simply by addressing what type of person you are when you are in it.

If you are happy and loving when you are with that person, then you probably have a healthy relationship. That is if you are looking at your relationship in an honest light, and if you really know what happiness is. Sometimes our perspective of the relationship is delusional. We may think we are happy and then find out later we weren't in our right minds.

If you find yourself being agitated or angered with this person frequently, then you might be in an unhealthy relationship. Again only you can assess your situation, because only you know what it is like to live with them. What others may see of your relationship on the outside, may be entirely different, than what you have to deal with when you two are alone. This type of situation occurs quite frequently.

You may find that friends or family might be baffled by the fact that you are experiencing frequent arguments. Keep in mind; if your partner acts differently in front of family and friends, it is all part of the façade. They want to make everything appear as if it is alright, even if on the inside, everything is falling apart.

This is another reason why it can be difficult to recognize the unhealthy behavior, because on one hand, you know what you are experiencing, but on the other hand, your friends and family are not validating your feelings. They don't see the behavior so in their minds it may not exist. This is where your intuition needs to override the influence of friends and family. Deciding whether a relationship is not good for you, rests in your hands.

Paying attention to the signs you experience will help you make that decision. If you do notice a personality change in yourself since you have entered the relationship, then you need to take a look at your compatibility. Sometimes relationships are very black and white, and the two involved are simply not compatible.

In an issue of being incompatible however, most people are able to recognize their incompatibility early on, and the relationship is very short lived. However, when two people cling on to the other's needs instead of assets, a dependency develops, whether the two are fully compatible or not. The relationship slowly evolves, but there are often signs of disagreements and unhealthy behaviors.

If you have ever talked to a friend about an unhealthy relationship, the phrases, "I should have known...," or "I knew right when...," usually come into conversation because you can actually see the warning signs. Seeing the warning signs is one thing, taking action and recognizing them is another.

One example of unhealthy behavior is control. We discussed the 'controller' role in our previous chapters, but now we will expand on the role and discuss the characteristics so you can recognize them. Control isn't always as obvious as the word itself. Control has a way of being subtle and gradual with its progression, and it differs from person to person.

For example, let's say you are with your partner and they start to exhibit jealous behavior. Well, maybe at first you are actually complimented by their gestures of jealousy, thinking that they are very interested in you as a person. However, jealousy is a form of control. There are cases where jealousy is an innocent expression and then there are instances where it is not. If jealousy invokes anger or abuse, whether verbal or physical, then it is not out of innocence, it is out of control. Any action that does not stem from love stems from the lack of love. Often people who are jealous lack self esteem, and become protective of the things that are not in their control. Partners are the closest target in their grasp.

Jealousy can be a gradual way to manipulate a partner's behavior. They may try to manipulate what friends you associate with or what type of places you go to through interrogation. You may even tend to avoid certain people or places just to avoid the argument. If you have the strength to recognize this behavior ahead of time, you will address the issue, and either resolve the behavior or leave the relationship.

Jealousy is often exhibited towards anyone the partner might feel threatened by or view as competition.. Again this is a reflection of your partner's insecurities in the relationship and themselves. Sometimes jealous behavior can be innocent and sometimes it can develop into a very unhealthy obsession. Listen to your instincts. If something doesn't feel right or feel good then your intuition is trying to tell you something. It is up to you to pay attention to these signals and act on them.

Extreme situations of jealousy can lead to rage, physical abuse, or obsessive behaviors. The partner might label their actions as 'love,' but they are not.

They might justify their actions by saying they just care so much, but this is not a healthy way to care for someone.

When we love or care for someone, we let them live. We let them experience life so that they can experience love. Love is not suffocating or isolating. It is an extension of who we are along with who we intend to be.

You have to have an idea of what love truly is otherwise you are susceptible to believing what others dictate love is to you. In our example of jealous behavior above, the partner justifies the unhealthy behavior by saying that they care, or that they love you. If your perspective of love was tainted, you might just believe that this is true. You may even believe that you need to stay with the relationship because this person 'cares' so much for you. You might fear that you might not find someone else to care this much for you, so you convince yourself to stay involved.

This is when you need to look at your own lack of love for yourself. Your self love is the foundation that you build all your relationships on. If a void exists and your self love is absent, you are prone to fill this need with outside sources, whether they are healthy or not. So even though your intuition may be functioning properly, and sending you warning signs of unhealthy behavior and relationships, the void inside yourself may overlook them and pursue the false sense of love.

Relationships are double-edged because not only do you need to recognize your partner's unhealthy behaviors, but you also need to recognize your own. Like attracts like, therefore sickness attracts sickness. So even though you may recognize some of the signs of unhealthy relationships, you have to pinpoint why you were attracted to them in the first place.

Here's a reference chart indicating some characteristics of healthy and unhealthy relationships:

Healthy Relationships	Unhealthy Relationships
Respects the partners choice of friends and family	Tries to prevent partner from being with others, even family members
Encourages one another to pursue their goals and be want they want to be in life	Degrades the others ideas, thoughts, or abilities, and tries to make them feel unworthy
Partner is confident and trusting about the relationship	Partner is threatened and exhibits jealous behavior
Partner allows other to carry on activities outside of their presence	Partner demands to know every move outside of their presence including the people involved
Partner trusts and respects your decisions	Partner questions everything you say and think
Partner makes you feel good. You enjoy their presence and feel open to be yourself.	Partner makes you feel insecure, depressed, and even anxious. You feel like you are walking on 'eggshells'
You rarely have arguments and if you do, they are settled easily	You have very frequent arguments and they result in yelling and even physical violence

You and your partner are willingly involved in the relationship. Either one could leave at any time and the other would accept the parting	Partner will not 'accept' a termination of the relationship and tries to provoke the other with guilt and/or following their whereabouts
Sexual encounters are a result of an agreement between both partners	Sexual encounters are sometimes forced or used as a form of manipulating their partner
Both partners in control of themselves and esteem	Primarily one person is in control over the other

This list by no means encompasses everyone's personal experiences with unhealthy relationships, but it does give you a side by side overview of some of the key characteristics.

Unhealthy relationships can often exhibit a distorted reality of sexual behaviors. In fact, sexual behaviors can actually be the only time both partners can 'communicate' without having a disagreement. But after a certain length of time even sexual situations can cause arguments. Sex can be used as a form of control instead of a form of love.

Partners in this type of unhealthy relationship find that if they were to remove the sexual relationship they have, there would be no relationship at all. There has to be something more in order to have a healthy foundation for a relationship. When sex becomes the livelihood of the relationship instead of the accessory, important characteristics of the relationship are overlooked.

The couple may center everything around their sexual desires and intentions instead of furthering an emotional connection. People with purely physical relationships can still carry on like a 'normal' couple, however their actions in private can be focused on sex as a perversity instead of sex as a part of love.

This type of relationship tends to work for a lot of different people who have had previous issues with sexual behaviors. To some extent, those that abuse sex may have been sexually abused. When someone is placed in a situation where they either have their choice of sex taken from them or misused, they are considered sexually abused. When this occurs, the control shifts over to the abuser. The victim can either respond in two ways; they can grow a fear of sexual relationships after the instance, or they can acquire a sexual obsession.

If the victim carries over their pain or emotions from the event in this manner, and it turns into a sexual obsession, there is no telling how long the pattern will continue in the person's life. The victim will always find relationships that satisfy their compulsion. They will continue to find relationships to satisfy their intense hunger, until the previous sexual abuse issues are dealt with.

So we are looking at two extremes, abstinence or obsession, whereas, a healthy relationship would be a balance in between the two. So also take note on what type of sexual relationships you have had with people. Make a confessional in your journal and write about some of your experiences. Don't focus so much on the physical pleasure, but the emotions behind the pleasure, if there were any at all. What sexual relationships were meaningful to you? Which ones were not? Analyze your behaviors and the behaviors of those you involved yourself with.

Some people think or associate sex alone as love and this is a misconception. Sex is simply an attribute of a relationship, not the core. It is a beautiful connection to experience, but it is also a responsibility between two people.

Control, jealousy, manipulation, guilt, and excessive anger are all tools for unhealthy relationships. The combination can be a deadly concoction. You should carefully assess your actions and the relationships you are in to see if any of these signs pertain to you. Recognizing the signs early on can save your health and sometimes even your life.

No one is immune to unhealthy relationships. They affect both men and women alike. Women can just as equally get angered and become physically abusive just like men. If the signs are there, the signs are there, gender is not a boundary.

It is more common for women to report abuse then it is for men. Often men fear coming forward because they think that they will not be believed by the proper authorities. The way our society focuses on men always being the aggressors it is understandable why abused men might feel this way.

According to The National Crime Victimization Survey (NCVS), there were 691,710 nonfatal violent victimizations committed by current or former spouses, boyfriends, or girlfriends of the victims during 2001. About 588,490, or 85% of intimate partner violence incidents, involved women. The offender in one fifth of the totality of crimes committed against women was an intimate partner - compared to only 3% of crimes committed against men.

These figures only account for the actual cases reported. They do not account for the many voices that remain silent. Rest assured there are many out there who have tucked away their pain, their emotions, and have moved on, whether resolving the pattern or not. If you are one of these people, it is vital for you to bring your feelings into awareness so that you can heal and move on towards a healthier life. Eliminate the pattern and let it end with you.

Get your journal out and start writing about any unhealthy behaviors you have experienced in your previous or current relationships. Start paying attention. Do you and your partner argue frequently over non-important matters? Make notes about the frequency. How is your health during this time? Are you suffering from headaches, anxiety, or depression? Start writing everything down so you can make the connections.

If you are assessing a current relationship and are concerned about your partner finding your journal, find a safe place for it. There is nothing worse then having the wrong person find your journal especially when you are trying so hard to use writing as a healthy outlet. For some people, a journal is their only voice. The last thing you want is your partner to find it, read it, and use it to fuel arguments. This journal is for your eyes only.

If you decide on down the line that you want to share your discoveries with your partner then that is fine. Just keep in mind what you are up against and use your intuition about it. If you are with someone that easily arouses their own anger, then you might want to discuss your journal in a counseling situation instead of one-on-one. Our primary concern is for your well-being and safety.

Exercise #5 Journal Entry Summary

1. What issues keep reappearing in your life? Do you keep entering relationships where you are trying to 'fix' or 'repair' someone? Do you keep choosing relationships where the relationship is one-sided?

2. What signs of unhealthy relationships ring true to you? Do you have other signs that are not listed in the example? What were they?

3. Make a confessional in your journal and write about some of your experiences. Don't focus so much on the physical pleasure, but the emotions behind the pleasure, if there were any at all. What sexual relationships were meaningful to you? Which ones were not? Analyze your behaviors and the behaviors of those you involved yourself with.

4. Do you and your partner argue frequently over non-important matters? Make notes about the frequency. How is your health during this time? Are you suffering from headaches, anxiety, or depression?

Exercise 6

Overcoming Fear & Anxiety

Being in any type of relationship where you have had to experience physical or emotional abuse takes a great deal of time to recover from. These types of relationships impose so much mental strain on our bodies and mind that we tend to experience an extreme sense of fear and anxiousness.

This fear stems from your body trying to warn you that you are in a dangerous situation. It's the best way your body knows how to tell you that there is something very serious going on with your well-being and your lifestyle. You can try to treat this anxiety or fear with prescribed medications or seek medical intervention, but until you actually step away from the situation that is tormenting you, the fear will remain.

Being with someone that makes you feel this way or causes this extreme sense of fear is not worth your health. Love is not fear. Nature has never intended you to feel confused, scared, or in a constant state of emotion while being in a relationship.

So often we think the problem stems from ourselves and ourselves alone. Our unhealthy partner may even try to convince us of this. What is sad is that you may just believe them because you place their opinion so high, even higher than your own. No one knows what is better for you than yourself. Listen to yourself. Listen to what your body is trying to tell you and take refuge for your own sense of sanity.

At this time you might think you are actually crazy. You may think that you are all alone in the situation and that your discomfort will continue forever. Relief comes when you are willing to get out, when you are willing to do what you need to, to be safe for yourself.

There are so many men and women that go through these feelings and emotions, they might think that this is the way they are suppose to live, but it doesn't have to be like that. You can get out. You don't have to try and make something work that obviously is not going to.

This fear you have is a very healthy one. It has great purpose for being there. It may not feel good to you at the time, but is your body's way of helping you into a better situation by making the current one very uncomfortable.

Trying to numb yourself from the fear or self-medicate with drugs, alcohol, or food will not help you. All that will do is prolong your situation by having you blindly stay in it. Your senses are there for a reason. A relationship that you have to numb yourself to be in, is not a valuable one.

Not only should you pay attention to this fear in relationships, but also with any other person or situation that you may encounter. You have a great intuition that lurks inside of you. If you practice using it often, it will eventually become a part of your daily life.

Everyone gives off an 'energy' that signals to us if we should be around them or not. Some people that are up to no good or might be very imbalanced may give you a funny feeling inside. Pay attention to that feeling as it will allow you to kind of steer your body and your relationships in the right direction. If something doesn't feel right or feel good then get away from it.

Work with your body. Work with your inner spirit. There really is a connection between the two. If someone's energy disturbs you, then chances are you shouldn't be around them. On the other hand, if someone's energy seems to be inviting, then an interaction between you two may be necessary.

The more you practice paying attention to your intuition's guidance, the better you will get at it. You will be amazed at the insight you will achieve. Your gut instinct is there for a very powerful reason. It is there to help guide you through life spiritually. It can be the hand that pulls you through the darkness and emerges you into light.

Take some notes as to what causes you fear in your life right now. Write it all down and then look at what you can do to alleviate this fear. Look at the cause or the root of the emotion. Is there something you are not admitting to yourself? Is there someone in your life that could be affecting you without you noticing? Or maybe you have had this experience in the past, recall your feelings and fears and write them down as well. The past is just as equally important to us here, as it helps us recognize the obstacles that prevent us from going forward.

Anxiety and fear go hand in hand. If you start to feel anxiety or panic attacks then something is really wrong with the situation and your body is throwing in a red flag, and trying to get you to listen up. Anxiety attacks are very difficult to deal with as they can affect all areas of your life.

You can become afraid to step out of your house. You can become afraid to do daily life activities such as going to a store, or going to work. Everything seems to become a chore and difficult to tolerate. A lot of people usually experience these attacks when they are going through a traumatic situation in their life.

Emotional and physical abuse can trigger anxiety. Sometimes people going through divorces or ending relationships can go through this emotion as well. Anxiety attacks usually subside after your body and mind are in the clear from the situation that caused them. However, some people do require medical attention if the severity is crippling to their lives, especially if suicidal tendencies or harm to others is present.

Make note though, medication is there for alleviation. It is not there for you to make it a solution to your problems. Some people may use medications to help them cope with the anxiety and yet still continue participating in the situation that caused them. That in itself is an unhealthy behavior as it prevents you from getting better and seeking safety.

Similar situations occur with anti-depressants. Instead of people looking at what is causing them unhappiness, they look for a quick fix or they think that something is medically wrong with how they feel. Your emotions are there to guide you in the right direction by giving you clues to what is best for you, and what is not best for you. Your body and mind work for you. They help you fine tune your functions daily, but you have to work with them. You have to listen.

If you do feel that you have a medical condition and that you need assistance, please do seek a doctor's advice, even if for just a physical examination. Especially in the instance of physical abuse, it would be wise to be completely checked out to make sure that there is nothing medical that is contributing to your health.

You can work your emotions out on paper. If you have fears or anxiety attacks, then log them in your journal. That way if you do need to seek a physician or counselor, then they will be able to better assist you, because the events are documented.

A lot of times people can make it through on their own, but if at any time you have doubts, then seek outside support or assistance. Sometimes once people reach an ultimate low in their relationship and start to become engulfed by this fear, they really don't know how to get out. They don't know what the problem is either, because they are too wrapped up with trying to cope with the fear.

The keyword is 'cope.' So often we try to just cope with our environment or our relationships instead of seeking higher ground. You don't always have to cope, and you don't always have to compromise yourself for the sake of another human being. You can cope with the fear or deal with it. You can cope with the situation that caused it or you can work towards getting out of it. The choice is really up to you.

Write about your fears and talk them over with someone you trust, preferably the person outside of the situation you are involved in. Have hope that this fear will pass when it is suppose to, and have faith just knowing that a solution can be made.

Exercise #6 Journal Entry Summary

1. Identify what fears you have in your life.

2. What do you think causes those fears?

3. When did these fears start?

4. Do you get anxiety?

5. Under what type of circumstances do you feel anxious?

6. How do you plan to help yourself with these feelings? Are you paying attention to your body's signal?

Exercise 7

To Stay or Go

If you are in an unhealthy relationship, sooner or later you will face the decision of whether you should stay or whether you should go. If you are unhappy in the relationship then either situation will initially cause you some emotional discomfort.

Nobody wants to hurt anybody, and that's why people stay in certain relationships so long, despite their unhappiness. Staying with someone however, just to be nice really isn't that kind of a gesture. First of all, if you are unhappy then no matter what you do to try and cover that unhappiness up, it will resurface.

If you are a parent, that unhappiness may come out on your children. If you are involved in a committed relationship, it may come out through infidelity. It may come out through anger or hostility toward your partner. Or it may come out as anger or destructive behavior towards yourself. And if you are the type of person that doesn't want to inflict any of your emotions onto others then you will likely start inflicting them onto yourself.

So when you are faced with the decision of whether you should stay or go, you need to take into consideration your own well being and the well being of others. Staying with someone just to please them is actually causing them more harm then if you left.

The most loving thing you can do for someone you care about, but don't want to be with is let go. By keeping a grip on someone you don't fully want to be with you are only preventing them from being in a relationship where the feelings are mutual.

Abusive partners usually do not go quietly if you are trying to get out of the relationship, so prepare for that ahead of time. The first stage is usually intense sadness or if at an extreme it might be anger. They may swear their love for you and follow up with gifts. They may start doing things that they promised they would do a long time ago. While these might seem like kind gestures, understand they are stemming from acts of desperation.

When you say you are leaving or thinking of breaking up, it is a sign to them that they are losing control over you. It is a sign that you are actually taking ownership of your life and emotions. For a controlling partner this may just be the closest thing to fear that they could get.

The second stage is usually guilt. Rest assured there will be phone messages, voicemails, or phone calls. This partner will go to any lengths to try and manipulate you into going back to the relationship. They might promise you all these changes. They might promise you a better life, but keep in mind abusive relationships don't have overnight solutions.

They might try to guilt you back into the relationship by saying lines like, 'I can't live without you,' or they may even threaten their own lives. Whatever they can say at this point, they will say. The truth is, they know you. They have had an abusive relationship with you so they know what makes you tick. And they know which buttons to push and what to say to make you move in their direction.

What they are doing is creating a vacuum that could easily suck you back in if you stand too close. First of all, if you are going to plan to leave someone in a live-in relationship, pack your bags while they are not there. Make sure you know they won't be home either. If you can, call a close friend and ask them to be with you while you are packing. A friend is good for the emotional support, but also for the security. You want to prepare for any unexpected visits from your partner and you want to be safe.

If you have the time to grab all your belongings that's great, but if you don't, only grab what you absolutely need. Keep in mind, you will probably not be returning to the location after you leave, so make this moment and this moment alone count.

If you have important financial papers around the location, be sure to grab them. You never know when an over zealous partner might seek revenge through your finances. Grab anything that is sentimental to you. If there is something that you have had for a long time, take it with you. Lastly, take your clothes. Everything else is only secondary and can easily be replaced as time goes on.

You are walking away with more than what you left... your well-being and your happiness. Even if you have to walk away without taking anything, you would still be better off than putting yourself in an emotionally or physically charged, abusive relationship.

After you have reached some sense of closure and had time to compose yourself, it is time to make a plan to cut yourself out of the relationship entirely. Quitting an abusive relationship can be like quitting any other type of addiction, you either do it cold turkey, or you are just dangling over the fence.

Follow up your words with actions. Don't say you are breaking up and then try to continue other aspects of the relationship such as sexual acts. Breaking up and getting out means you are severing the ties to all aspects of the relationship. Also keep in mind sex can be used as a form of control, so recognize that for what it is, however tempting it may be.

There are people who try to rekindle abusive relationships after they leave the situation. You might think, "things weren't so bad," or "things have changed now." The truth is, abusive relationships may have a brief break for a month or two, but they will eventually wind up right back where they started, dead ends.

On-again, off-again relationships can go on for years with intermissions in between. Sometimes two people can grow together, but sometimes they grow apart. Once you cut off the relationship, make a note to yourself in your journal about how you feel right at that moment. Write down why you are breaking the relationship up so in case you ever try and return to it, you have a written reminder to yourself.

People do change, but they have to want to. Emotional and physical abuse do not heal themselves over night, neither do the patterns that created them. So use common sense when you are being approached to rekindle the unhealthy relationship. The first time you are involved with someone and they inflict abuse onto you, it is their fault. The second time you choose to be involved with them after knowing their behavior, it is your fault.

If you are unsure of your situation, and unsure of whether you want to release the relationship or not, then do nothing at all. Stillness can be an action all on its own. If you have uncertainty and need to research your own feelings then give yourself time to do so. If you are not being physically harmed then you can give yourself 3-6 months to see if the relationship changes.

You have to at least communicate to your partner the changes you would like to see occur. Don't expect someone to make a change without even knowing what it is. If they are willing to work on themselves and the relationship then you can give them

3-6 months to actually follow through. If you do not see a change and you are still dissatisfied with the relationship, then you have your answer.

This time frame is not necessarily one that you want to communicate to your partner, it is for you. You may come to a conclusion about the relationship prior to the 3-6 months and that is perfectly acceptable. The point is that you do not have to rush yourself if you are unsure of what measures to take. This time line can be especially useful for abusive marriages that have been going on for years or decades. The principles are still the same. However, there are complications involved; finances, children, and division of joint belongings.

Your answers will come to you once you are able to identify your feelings and the situation you are involved in. Again it is not advisable to stay in a physically or sexually abusive relationship even if you are unsure about leaving. Physical harm is a severity that requires your action to get out of the situation. Every second counts in these relationships so use your time wisely and get out before it's too late.

If you want to sort out your thoughts and feelings, write them down. Make a column about why you would want to leave the relationship and then make a separate column as to why you would want to stay. If one column has more than the other then you have an idea of what answer you are leaning towards.

Be honest to yourself here. Don't just write down what you think you would like to see or hear. Write down the reality of your relationship and identify any behaviors that you feel contribute to your decision. Look at your partner for what they truly are to you and what role they play in your life.

If you do choose to leave the relationship, write down your plan of action. This is especially important if your safety is involved. Not only think about how you are going to leave, but also make a plan as far as where you will go. Do you have the finances to support yourself and get your own place? Or is there a close friend or family member that you can safely stay with? If you don't have either resource, is there a shelter that you can go to locally?

Keep your journal in a safe place where the partner cannot find it. This is a tip for your safety. In an emotional or physical abuse relationship, you can feel like every move of yours is being monitored and usually your suspicions are right. Your journal is your outlet. It's a place where you can gather your senses and try to organize the situation into manageable size.

You might not feel comfortable talking to family members about your situation. You may not even be ready to talk to friends. So it is vital for you to talk to yourself through journaling. Writing can keep you sane in an insane situation so use it to your advantage and towards your healing. Your answers and strength will come to you when they are supposed to.

Some people involved in abusive relationships are so afraid to leave that they would rather lose their own life than walk away. This is perhaps the most desperate of thoughts. Losing your life over another person is not an option, it is an excuse to not stand up for yourself.

If you are feeling suicidal then seek professional help or tell someone you trust about it. Let this be a wakeup call to you. Your life doesn't need to end, but the relationship that is causing you to feel this way does. Open your eyes to what you are going through and be your own best friend here. Give yourself advice like you would a close friend you really care about. Give yourself hope and know that there is a safe way out of a relationship. You just have to be willing to walk away.

You may feel like you owe your partner an explanation or that you owe them something in general. This is not always the case. If giving an explanation for leaving may pose a threat to you physically or emotionally then leave first, explain later. Once you are physically removed from the situation, then you can opt to communicate through other means than in person. This can prove to be especially useful if the partner is easily angered or provoked.

You could even write a letter to them or call them if you wanted. What is amazing is abusers often totally overlook that anything was even wrong. They might be entirely oblivious to all the grief that you had to endure. So they may press you for explanations, when in actuality, they don't see the abuse because they choose not to.

In a healthy relationship, you would be able to explain your decision one-on-one with your partner, because in a healthy relationship both partners are coming from a sane train of thought. When you are dealing with leaving an unhealthy relationship you have to understand that the person you are dealing with might not be on a mentally safe ground. They might react insanely when posed with the right ignition. Losing control over you, could be just that ignition. That is why we are focusing on eliminating that opportunity for them to cause you harm.

Focus on yourself and the needs you have. Remember to not stay in the relationship simply because you are trying to protect the person from harm or suffering. Use your intuition and know when enough is enough. If you are unsure and want to try the relationship a little longer to see if things change, give yourself a timeline and stick to it. If things don't work or if there are no improvements in the relationship, then accept your results and make plans to move on.

Exercise #7 Journal Entry Summary

1. Make a column about why you would want to leave the relationship and then make a separate column as to why you would want to stay. If one column has more than the other then you have an idea of what your answer is.

2. If you do choose to leave the relationship, write down your plan of action. This is especially important if your safety is involved. Not only think about how you are going to leave, but also make a plan as far as where you will go. Do you have the finances to support yourself and get your own place? Or is there a close friend or family member that you can safely stay with? If you don't have either resource, is there a shelter that you can go to locally?

Exercise 8

Signs of Healthy Relationships

In our previous exercises, we discussed some of the signs of unhealthy relationships and we lightly touched some of the characteristics of healthy relationships in our comparison chart. Now we are going to go into some of the signs of healthy relationships in more detail, as the two may be difficult to decipher if you have never been taught the difference.

You can really be oblivious to what makes up a healthy relationship if you have only encountered unhealthy ones. It is as if you are coming out of a sheltered world and seeing light for the first time. It can be an amazing feeling, but overwhelming if you have no idea what healthy love can feel like.

In fact, you may have to go through several healthy relationships just to gain a better understanding on how things operate. Let's use an example so that we can look at how easily a healthy relationship can flow. Let's say you have entered a relationship that is loving, trusting, and giving. Both parties respect one another's thoughts and feelings. You enjoy one another's company for several months with little disagreements at all.

Eventually, the relationship reaches a point where it feels as though the two of you have drifted far apart. Perhaps you feel as though this relationship can no longer go on. You discuss it with your partner and decide to break up as a result. You go your separate ways or you may remain friends with one another.

Now this is a basic example of how a healthy relationship might flow into sequence. Granted there are many complexities that can occur with even a healthy relationship, but we are just using a simple example. Had this had been an unhealthy relationship, the situation may have unfolded like this:

You enter into an unhealthy relationship. You experience some conflicts with each other right from the start, yet continue to pursue one another. You have very little in common. You don't know if this person is truly being honest with you half the time or not. You both exhibit insecurities about the relationship. Months pass and the relationship progresses, but so do the disagreements. You decide to discuss getting out of the relationship. Your partner doesn't agree with your decision and pursues you relentlessly.

You feel guilty because your partner is showing what you think is 'love' and you opt to try the relationship again. A month or so later you are encountering the same issues and are now experiencing more frustration and unhappiness. The cycle keeps repeating until you physically and emotionally remove yourself from the relationship.

This is an example of how an unhealthy relationship unfolds. There is no flow because we have two people on separate plains trying to interact with one another. The connection may be there in small interests, but overall, the partners have different goals and are going in two separate directions.

Healthy relationships, on the other hand have a certain flow to them. There is a unity present even though there are two separate people coming together. Both partners are able to evenly flow interchangeably through each others lives because they respect one another's sense of being.

A partner in a healthy relationship doesn't expect you to overly compromise yourself or your family. They allow you to continue living the way you see fit. They respect the time you need with others including friends or families. They do not try to control who you are within or outside of the relationship.

A healthy relationship allows you to grow without boundaries. It allows you be what you want to be without worrying about having to please others' expectations of you. A healthy relationship is a balanced one. It means that you both give to the relationship equally. You spend time putting into the relationship not, taking out.

A healthy relationship is when two people compliment one another in their ideas, their lifestyles, in work and in play. It doesn't mean that both partners must mirror one another's actions, it just means that they can work together even if their characteristics are different.

There is an amazing amount of care that you can experience when you enter a relationship that is healthy. Even though you may carry some of your worry from previous relationships with you, as the trust you both share grows, the worry subsides.

True love is kind and patient with not only our strengths but also our weaknesses. Everyone has sore spots that they don't even know exist until they enter a relationship. You discover some of your best imperfections when you are with a good partner, mainly because there is someone there to watch all your behaviors. Your partner gets to see all angles of your private life. They get to see you happy, mad, sad, shy and even scared.

They get to see you do some of the silliest things. They get to share laughter and love. They catch all your little fascinations and interests. You get the opportunity to share so much with your partner in a healthy relationship because you are not spending all your time arguing or worrying. All the disagreements and concerns take time out of all the joy a good partner has to offer you.

Exercise #8 Journal Entry Summary

1. Write down what you feel is a healthy relationship.

2. Write down what you would want in your partner. Think about what you would like to share with them. Think about all the different things you would like to do together.

3. What was the closest thing you had to a healthy relationship? What made it healthy to you?

Exercise 9

Awareness

When you start living your life with awareness, you will discover there is no turning back. The old shoe will no longer fit because you know there is something better out there, a better way of life. Although unhealthy patterns may be the most comfortable, you will no longer be able to live in such darkness no matter how hard you try.

Awareness is one of the most enlightening experiences in the world, but it can be the hardest to face and make transition to. You have to understand that these patterns that you have in your life have been chiseled away for probably years. It would be unimaginable to resolve all your life issues in a day. You have to practice living healthier and wiser.

You have to live consciously and take a good look at your actions and those around you. You can't change your past or the people that were involved in it, but you can change yourself and the future you choose to be a part of.

Awareness is essentially an awakening of your mind, body, and spiritual connection. This is the moment when you pay attention to what you are thinking, feeling, and living instead of just walking blindly.

When we start taking back control over our own lives, we are able to live in freedom. We are able to step away from our past issues and go beyond them. You have taken the time to look at your issues, your relationships, and the emotions that surrounded them. Now it is time to live a life of awareness, a mindful life.

Be aware of what your wants and needs are so that you know what it is you want before you involve yourself in a relationship. Assess your own needs. Take out your journal and dedicate a section to your needs and wants in a relationship. Feel free to be specific, as if you were placing a custom made order.

Think about what you want in a partner and then write about it. Do you want happiness? Then write about what makes you happy. Raise your self esteem here and write about what you would want if you could have anything you wanted in a companion.

When you work on your issues it is a process. Those issues have such an impact on your well-being and your self-esteem. Perhaps you never sought a healthy relationship because you didn't feel as though you deserved one. This idea is one that needs to be banished from your being.

Everyone is entitled to happiness and therefore entitled to have a healthy relationship. However, they have to be willing to do the footwork to re-teach themselves a healthy lifestyle and way of thinking. You can't do wrong to yourself and expect to attract a healthy relationship. Granted it happens, but if you are too wrapped up in your own short-comings, you probably won't even realize a relationship's goodness, even if it is right in front of your face.

You have to 'be' what it is you 'want.' If you want a healthy relationship then you have to be healthy. Take for example, you want a partner who is a non-smoker and enjoys exercising, but you smoke and don't exercise. Well, your first step would be to quit your unhealthy behaviors and stop smoking and begin some form of exercise. Point being, you can't expect your partner to be or do something you wouldn't do yourself.

Recognizing unhealthy relationships is only part of the equation. You have to repair yourself in the process. You have to be aware of your own personal value. If you think that something within yourself needs to be changed then you need to put some of your extra energy into changing it.

View this as preparing yourself for something beautiful, being united with a companion that equally contributes to themselves as part of the whole. Invest in yourself here. Write down in your journal what you would like to change in yourself. Be honest with yourself and write down your faults or behaviors you would like to change. This is your personal assessment. You are cleaning out your emotional closet and your physical closet too.

Earlier, you were asked to focus on your past issues. Now you are being asked to just look at yourself for what you really are. In order to attract healthy relationships, you need to be healthy. Health comes from the inside and transpires to the outside. If you don't feel good about who you are then it is going to affect the type of relationships you feel you are worthy of entering.

It's important to recognize your worth, your personal value. You do have a lot to offer, but if you don't believe that to be true then the thought does not become an action.

Now that you have written down what habits or behaviors you would like to change about yourself, you need to assess your good qualities. Everyone has good qualities no matter what their self esteem tells them on the inside. So start another section, title it whatever you like and start listing some of your good qualities. If this exercise is difficult for you, then you have a lot of work to do with your self esteem.

If you are coming from a history of unhealthy relationships it is understandable why your self esteem has been damaged. Be patient with yourself and work on journal exercises such as the one discussed above. You have to get out of the mind frame that you are not worthy. This form of thought does not benefit you. You don't have to hide in the dark anymore. You can stand tall and be proud of what you have to offer.

Some people feel ashamed, especially if they have had abusive relationships, either sexually, physically, or emotionally. Your feelings are very valid and you are not alone with having them. You can get through this and come out of the situation with more than what you left. This is not about giving in, it's about standing up for yourself and realizing that you do not have to stay down simply because of how someone made you feel.

That moment in your life is isolated in time. It will not be repeated unless you allow it to be. Some situations are out of our control, and others are in our control, if we have the necessary awareness. Your goal is to build yourself up and be accounted for. You can protect yourself by being aware of what situations you involve yourself in.

We create a force field of strength when we believe in who we are and what we stand for. Know your truth and you will know no harm. Obstacles may come your way, but you will be able to face them with a renewed sense of self and perspective. Take pride in the qualities that make you, 'you.' Write down things that you may even secretly like about yourself. Maybe it is the way you smile or maybe it is the way you take time listening to others.

If you are having trouble making this list then maybe you need to focus on what or where you acquired such a low perspective of yourself. Again, use this as an opportunity to write in your journal. This will allow you to retrace your steps mentally to see where the root of the problem may be. Did someone tell you that you weren't good enough? Or was there an argument within a relationship that may have made you feel like you were not worthy?

This is an opportunity to reclaim that which is yours… the 'heart.' Your self esteem may have never been recovered from childhood wounds. Really look beyond the surface and track down the thorn in your paw. Write it all out. Get whatever it is that may be bothering you out onto the white space before you. You can look at the situation for what it truly is and then release its power over you.

Almost everyone has insecurities or self-esteem issues they need to work through. So you are not alone if you are dealing with them. Just be patient with yourself and you will be able to come out on top.

Either way, take time to work on writing your list of good qualities about yourself. It is important that you do not overlook this exercise, as it is a symbol of what you believe in yourself. Take as long as you want to complete it, but make it a part of your conscious awareness.

Living a life of awareness means that you are willing to live truthfully. Once you accept this truth into your life, you will no longer be able to avoid it. It will become a part of who you are and the life you choose to lead.

Exercise #9 Journal Entry Summary

1. Dedicate a section to your needs and wants in a relationship. Feel free to be specific, as if you were placing a custom made order.

2. Think about what you want in a partner and then write about it. Do you want happiness? Then write about what makes you happy. Raise your self esteem here and write about what you would want if you could have anything you wanted in a companion.

3. Write down in your journal what you would like to change in yourself. Be honest with yourself and write down your faults or behaviors you would like to change. This is your personal assessment. You are cleaning out your emotional closet and your physical closet too.

4. Make a separate section and list your good qualities. Be thorough in your descriptions.

Exercise 10

Recovery

Relationships can cripple our concepts of reality and leave us with distorted outlooks on life. Depending on how serious the damage, scars can remain even though the relationship is no longer active. All forms of abuse can affect us, but some more than others.

Emotional abuse is often hard for people to recognize or even describe because it is a form of mental manipulation where one usually has power over the other. This form of abuse is always difficult for someone to communicate to others, as there is no physical evidence of its presence, unless it has gone on long enough to affect someone's health.

If you have had one of these relationships, your partner might have convinced you to not mention the occurrences to others close to you. Your partner might insist your disagreements or arguments are not 'others' business.' This is a form of control exhibited by your partner, as they are trying to prevent you from getting help. As long as you stay inside their little world they created for you, they will have full control. This could be one of the loneliest worlds you ever enter.

Silence does not benefit you here. If something feels wrong, then speak out to someone you trust. Maintain those trusted ties as they are the ties that might help you remember a somewhat 'normal' way of life.

You can recover from emotional abuse by first recognizing it, either in your past or in the present. If you are still in the situation, then you need to assess the reasons why. Don't commit to the idea that you have to learn to deal with emotional abuse, or learn to live with it for that matter. No one has to live that way. Even if it is your family, or another loved one, you don't have to stay in a situation that does not benefit your well-being.

Some people try to wait for a 'change' to take place in their partner, but it doesn't happen. That person has to want to change. Simply saying that they want to change is not enough. They have to take action. Otherwise, things will be alright for a month or so, then be right back to where you were, in the same isolated world you started out in.

Try to dedicate a half way point for yourself. Most emotional abuse heightens when the partners live together. If this happens to be your situation then maybe you need to take your belongings and stay somewhere else, either with a relative, a close friend, or your own place. If you reach your hands out for help, there will be someone or some way to help pull you through, have faith in that.

Follow through with your actions after you have reached a separation. Set some boundaries for yourself. Most people try to save the relationship regardless of the damage committed, mainly because they are holding on to merely the concept of being in a relationship, and not the actual purpose of having one.

If you think your partner is committed or open enough to make a change, then discuss what areas in your relationship you feel are unhealthy. Keep in mind we cannot always mold our partner to be the person we want them to be. You can only expect someone to change so much. Realize that some characteristics are just part of their being and you may be better off releasing the relationship.

There are instances where two people are able to grow together through unhealthy situations, but both partners must be willing to commit to the effort required to work on themselves. Sometimes this works and sometimes it doesn't.

Recovery begins when the situation that disturbs you ends. At that point you are able to collect yourself and gather your senses. When you step outside your situation, you are able to see things you may have not realized before.

No matter what your situation was, you will never go away empty handed. You may have to leave material items. You may have to leave your own comfort zone, but you are going to walk away with much more. Every time we have to endure any form of discomfort, we gain strength from the situation and an understanding of compassion for others.

However, some people turn their experience into something much harsher. They may take their discomfort and turn it inward by harming themselves. Instead of striving to rise above the situation, they may strive to relive the event, perhaps subconsciously, because the issue was never resolved.

They may turn their feelings and emotions into obsessive behaviors towards foods, drugs, or even sexual behaviors. Anything that the person can do to feel as though the tables are turned and they are in control, they will do. Whether they are aware of the behavior or not, they will continue to put their emotions inward. The pattern of self defeat could continue years and years after the actual emotional incident occurred.

Some people may suppress their emotions and then turn them in to anger or hate. They may even become recluse and develop depression over something that occurred long ago.

When this happens, you let them win. You let everyone that ever presented harm to you, win. Instead of recognizing the power that you do have, you chose to continue to allow them to control you even though the situation has ended.

Recovery begins when you reclaim yourself. It begins when you stand up and take notice that you are worth something better than what you have been handed. It begins when you believe in yourself and the experiences that make you what you are at this very moment.

Raise your head up. You need bow down to no one. You need not be told how to feel, how to love, or how to live your life. All you need to do is put one foot in front of the other and walk. Realize that you have the strength to build a better life for yourself and your family, simply by sticking up for yourself. You have a voice and you deserve to be heard.

If you are recovering from physical or sexual abuse in an unhealthy relationship or situation then you are certainly not alone. [5]According to *Rape in America: A Report to the Nation*, there are 1.3 adult women being forcibly raped every minute. This means that 78 women are forcibly raped each hour, and 1,871 women are forcibly raped every day. The figures are just daunting and a frightening indication of the types of unhealthy behaviors that exist as well.

Most people that become physical or sexual abusers have been abused themselves. This is a perfect example of a person not dealing with past issues or recognizing their patterns in life. They relate to their victims in the same manner that they were shown. They repeat the past instead of recognizing it. Again, those that were not shown love, were shown the lack of love.

By no means does this justify the behavior of an abuser, however it does allow us to identify their sickness. No one chooses to be assaulted or physically harmed, unless it is an instance of self abuse. Physical and sexual abuse often occurs from the people the person knows. It might be a family member, either immediate family or distant. It may be a friend of the family or a friend of someone's friend. There is usually some type of link back to someone that person knows.

Then there is the random act of violence and abuse where the abuser does not know the victim. They just prey upon anyone accessible to them at the time. Either instance, whether you know the abuser or not, you have entered into an unhealthy relation with them. You may not want to think of this as a form of a relationship, but it is an interaction no matter how unhealthy it may be.

Physical and sexual abuse leaves not only physical markings but also emotional. It wrecks a person's self esteem and takes away something they hold so dear to them, their personal boundaries. When someone inflicts harm onto our personal and physical being, they cross a line of defense. What is left after the incident is a memory that might repeat itself over and over in the victim's head.

If this form of abuse has occurred in your life, you need to forgive yourself. You need to know that this is not your fault. You did not cause the incident nor were you able to control it. Sometimes no matter how safe we would like to think that we are, physical and sexual abuse can make its way into our lives. For whatever reason, we were chosen to have these experiences in our lives, but the important thing is that you are walking away with something from the event... your life.

If you are fortunate enough to have been able to walk away from the event, then you will be fortunate enough to have the opportunity to recover emotionally and physically. There are many people out there that were not given such an opportunity. So, despite the difficulty that you had to face, all is not lost.

Recovering from unhealthy relationships no matter what their nature, takes time and patience. You have to be patient with yourself and be loving just like you would a friend or family member. Believe that there is a solution, that no situation no matter how overwhelming is permanent. Our lives can change dramatically from one day to the next.

Have faith that you need tackle only this moment in time. You don't have to worry about what will come tomorrow or how you will feel for that matter. Just focus on what you can do for yourself right now. Give yourself a kind and gentle hand as you work through the issues and situations you have faced in life.

See yourself as a whole person, not just the fragments and pieces you are trying to place back together. While you are dealing with your recovery, take time to write. Every time you feel anger or sadness, grab a pen or pencil and write. Make use of your emotions and put them to work. You will eventually find a good use for them later.

The important thing is that you are in a safe place. If you are in an unhealthy relationship and don't feel as though you have the strength to get out, start opening up. Go to either a close friend or family member and be honest and tell them what is going on. If you don't have a close friend or family member that you can contact then get involved in either counseling or support groups. The help is there, you just have to be willing to look for it.

Just talking to others about what you are dealing with can help validate the feelings you are having. Sometimes we don't realize everything we are dealing with until we actually discuss it with others. Stuffing your emotions doesn't help you solve the problem it only prohibits you from the solution. You will make it through whatever you are going through and you will come out on top of the situation.

Exercise #10 Journal Entry Summary

1. Write down your thoughts and feelings during your steps towards recovery.

2. Make plans for what you can do to help ease any discomfort you have with your emotions. This will help you use positive outlets instead of negative.

3. Talk to a close friend or seek a counselor if necessary. It helps to have someone validate your emotions and this in turn will help you heal.

4. Relax and meditate on everything that has surfaced. Each day will get easier. Just keep doing what is best for you.

Exercise 11

Rebuilding Trust

When we are recovering from unhealthy relationships we start to realize that we missed out on a lot of experiences that healthy relationships have. One major characteristic is trust. Trust is such a hard trait to establish in any relationship and even more so if our idea of trust was damaged from prior relationships. We carry with us a fear of trusting someone we are close to because we are afraid of that trust being broken again.

This is a very healthy fear to have, after all, we are trying to make better choices for ourselves and the relationships that we involve ourselves in. We do have to protect our best interest and not be so naïve to the fact that others don't always have our well being at heart. However, there will come a time when we meet someone that we are actually able to open up to and begin to rebuild some of our issues with trust. This event will be a very interesting time for anyone who has had several unhealthy relationships as it will be a breath of fresh air. This moment may come soon after an unhealthy relationship, or it may come after years of self exploration. Whenever the time comes, be confident and know that this is practice for you to experience aspects of a healthy relationship. Any new way of life takes practice. As you begin entering healthier relationships, you will acquire this new way of living no matter how awkward this may feel.

After we have spent so much time in unhealthy life situations and events, we have to dedicate ourselves to re-learning a healthier and better way of life. When we are actually ready for this experience, we magically start having opportunities being presented to us. We might meet someone that is completely different from the type of person we are familiar to associating with.

This moment will baffle us and maybe even mesmerize us at the same time. Don't give up, no matter how uncomfortable this healthy relationship may be. Be open to a change and you will be open to your own happiness.

Sometimes the best thing to do in this type of situation is to be honest with the person you are involving yourself with. Tell them that you have had some difficult relationships and that this type of relationship is very new to you. If you feel comfortable with them and you have some level of trust, you may even be able to talk about some of your prior experiences. You don't have to get extremely personal with someone right away. Give yourself time to develop some level of confidence in your new relationship.

Sometimes when we expose ourselves too early on in the relationship we leave ourselves open to vulnerability. So, feel it out and see if this person opens up to you. Then see if you are able to reach out to one another on a common level. When we discuss our previous issues in life, not all people are able to feel comfortable with our pasts. That is mainly due to the fact that they don't feel comfortable with their own pasts.

If this is a truly healthy relationship then you will be able to feel like you can say anything to one another. Healthy relationships are about being mutual, not about being one-sided. It takes two people to work as a team. Teams were not created by one person alone. When you develop a partnership, you have to be able to feel like you can trust someone and that trust can take time.

Trust is apparent in so many daily life activities and yet we tend not to realize it. Especially when you are coming from an unhealthy relationship, you may feel like very simple daily life events were taken out of proportion due to the lack of trust. For example, say your partner had promised that they were going to be in a certain place at a certain time and never showed up. Well, your trust in them was broken. You may have forgiven them and then opted to try it again, only to become disappointed when the same instance occurred.

This is an example of a very simple event, but it actually destroyed your trust because this person was unable to be honest with you. Once these instances happen over and over again, you no longer feel like you can depend on that person and therefore there is a link broken in that partnership.

When you have a healthy relationship, you can trust that that partner will be there when they say they will. You can trust that they are not lying to you, cheating on you, or providing you with a distorted reality of who they really are.

No matter who you begin your healthy relationship with, trust doesn't happen overnight. So take one step at a time and enjoy the new discoveries you encounter together. Be willing to learn a new way of loving and sharing yourself with someone else.

To help you learn a little more about yourself and what you think trust is, take a moment to write down your definition. Make a section in your notebook dedicated to 'trust.' Write down all the people you have trusted. Talk about whether you continue to trust them now or if your trust was broken by them. If you still trust them now, write about why. If you don't trust them, write about what happened that broke your trust.

Write about what your expectations are in a partner that you would like to trust. Then take a look at yourself. Are you an honest person? Write about what makes you worthy of someone's trust. Do you trust yourself?

If you are accustomed to being with people that are not trust worthy then being with someone you can trust is just incredible. People that are used to unhealthy relationships will often continue to exhibit some of their same behaviors. For example, let's say you are used to your partner always staying out late and coming home at odd hours. Well, you might just continue to think that every other partner you have might do the same thing, so basically if you worried then, you may also exhibit worry now.

This is very natural and will subside as you rebuild your sense of trust with both relationships and people in general. If you have an understanding and patient partner then you should try discussing any fears that you have before you get too involved. This way you can also get an idea where your partner is coming from as well.

Learning to trust again will happen eventually. One of the most beautiful gifts in the world is when the universe hands you something you didn't know you were ready for. So pay attention to its calling. You will know when the opportunity is right.

Exercise #11 Journal Entry Summary

1. Make a section in your notebook dedicated to 'trust.' Write down all the people you have trusted. Talk about whether you continued to trust them now or if your trust was broken by them. If you still trust them now, write about why. If you don't trust them, write about what happened that broke your trust.

2. Write about what your expectations are in a partner that you would like to trust. Then take a look at yourself. Are you an honest person? Write about what makes you worthy of someone's trust. Do you trust yourself?

Exercise 12

Trying Again

The *Americans for Divorce Reform* estimates that "*Probably, 40 or possibly even 50 percent of marriages will end in divorce if current trends continue. However, that is only a projection and a prediction.*"[6] That means that there are a lot of relationships out there that don't work out. So if you thought you were, by chance, the only one that was having some bad luck with partners, you were mistaken.

Just think, this statistic doesn't include breakups or common law marriages. Anyone that is willing to go out onto the playing field and try entering into a relationship, has to realize that you don't always get a home run the first time around. Sure, it would be wonderful if we could fall into the arms of our soul mate the first time we start to date someone, but that doesn't always happen.

Most of the times, we have to experience some trial and error. In one of our exercises you were asked to write about what you wanted in a partner. You were asked to do this because often at times people don't know what they want. They just go out and grab anything that responds to them at the time and that's it. In all honesty, you deserve to be picky.

If you were told right at this moment you had to pick a partner that you would be with for this lifetime, chances are you would stop and think about the type of person you want to be with. Other times you have to learn what type of person you would want to be with by getting out and gaining experiences with others.

Some people have to date multiple people and some people have to have multiple marriages in their lifetime. Regardless of how many times you have gone out there and tried to have a successful relationship and it did not work, don't be afraid to try again.

Some people find their life's partner at 20, some 30, even 60 and above. Age does not prohibit you from being loved or loving someone else. As long as you have taken a good look at the patterns evolved from your previous relationships, you can change the way you deal inside a relationship and actually be successful.

Of course, you can't build a relationship out of dirt. You do need to have the right partner for you. Don't expect to pick a different face with the same traits you found before in failed relationships and expect to have an entirely different outcome. Get rid of your old shoes, especially if they don't fit who you are anymore.

Our relationships change because we change. Sometimes two people can evolve together and sometimes it requires them to be apart. It is okay that you have had previous relationships. It does not mean that you are a failure and do not deserve to be loved. It just means that you were not ready nor was the person you might have been involved with.

Don't settle for second best, go out there and find what you want. Don't just try to force things to work or compromise who you are. If you enter a relationship and it doesn't work out, accept that and move on. You don't have to give up and commit your life to solitude. You are entitled to try again.

You deserve to be happy. You deserve to have someone in your life that does care for you as much as you care for them. You deserve to be treated properly. You deserve the experience of having a relationship that adds to your life, not subtracts from it.

Once you recognize your behavior and you are ready to set some personal boundaries for yourself and whomever you involve yourself with, then you can go out and try again. Try a practice round on paper first. Use your journal and dedicate a section to 'personal boundaries.' You may not even know what your personal boundaries are. If you don't, then it is kind of hard to reinforce them in a relationship. Writing your boundaries down first is a good way to try out your ideas.

Boundaries are personal shields that you set up for yourself. It's basically like setting up a line that you don't want people to cross except this line is a mental one. When you know your boundaries, you know your own personal rules that you have for yourself and for the people that you involve yourself with.

Some examples of boundaries are as follows; You do not want to be with someone that is a smoker, You do not want to be with someone that doesn't have time for you, You don't want to be with someone that travels a lot, or You don't want to be with someone that can't be monogamous, or You don't want to be with a drinker. You set up your own guidelines of what you will handle and what you will not handle.

Personal boundaries are just that…personal. They are there for you to make and for you to stick to. Part of setting up mental boundaries means that you also have to reinforce them verbally to your partner. Sticking to your boundaries is a way of double checking yourself from getting involved in another unhealthy relationship. When you start learning how to experience love in a different way, you have to run through your checklist to review what you initially wanted. Your partner might be real close to your list of wants or they may be far off. So be sure to refer back to your journal entry where you had to list the type of person you want to be with. As time progresses in the relationship, you can refer to your boundary list and see if you have allowed some of your rules to become crossed or if you stuck to them.

If one of your boundaries has become crossed, it is your responsibility to communicate this to your partner. If the person really respects your boundaries then they will work with you on it, or maybe you can both come up with a reasonable compromise. Not all personal rules need to be compromised though so keep that in mind. It's ok to have some personal boundaries that you never want crossed. Remember the boundaries you feel the strongest about and stick with them. You have chosen them for a reason.

If you are creating a personal boundary list before you actually become involved in a relationship, then that is great, because we can tend to compromise our beliefs if we are struck by love's opportunity. Our views can become foggy and misguided. So if you have a list pre-written of your boundaries, you can go back and check yourself to make sure you are abiding to your own rules.

Entering into a new relationship after having an unhealthy one can be very scary at first. If your trust was broken and you had to deal with a rollercoaster of a relationship, you have every reason to be shy of starting over. If you begin a new relationship after months or years of time elapsed and say by chance the new relationship doesn't work out, you may really be apprehensive to try again.

Your feelings are valid. Just take your time. There is no rush. Let love happen to you, but prepare yourself in the meantime for the discovery. You may feel as though you are protecting yourself from being harmed, by closing people out, but don't forget, you are also protecting yourself from being loved.

As long as you have done the exercises in our previous chapters about dealing with your own issues and recognizing the signs of unhealthy relationships, then you have the tools you need to try again. When you allow love to unfold by its own hands, you will be amazed at what you are presented.

Exercise #12 Journal Entry Summary

1. Create a section in your journal called 'personal boundaries.' Begin by listing some of your personal boundaries that you have or want to have in a relationship.

2. If you have concerns about trying a relationship again, write down your fears or questions. Then try to come up with your own answers. Work through the issues instead of allowing them to stand in your way.

Exercise 13

Turn Darkness to Light

Having unhealthy relationships or difficult situations happen to you in life does not go to waste. Any situation we had occur in our life only adds to our experience as a person. It's not about what happens to you in life; it's about what you make happen.

You can allow situations to hold you down or you can allow them to pick you up. If we drop the idea of being a 'victim', we can use our experience to benefit our understanding of ourselves and those around us. The experience itself that you have gained from having unhealthy situations occur in life does not go untouched.

You may be able to use your experience to help others either directly or by example. You can make use of your pain by coming out on top of it. Sometimes we can allow ourselves to become so involved in where we are that we forget who we are. And that 'who' we are is always there despite of what we go through.

It is quite comparable to a flower. You have the stem, the center, and the petals. That flower may have all of its petals pulled off one by one, its beauty taken, but it still lives on through that center. And that center is what keeps us going through the difficult moments in life where we struggle to think of better days.

You can either allow your experiences to consume you or you can use them to pursue you. Don't let your pain be an excuse for self-destruction. Nothing is more hypocritical than when someone inflicts the same pain they experienced onto themselves or other people.

For example, if you were a child of an alcoholic and you grew up in a difficult family environment that had affected you deeply, then why would you want to inflict the same environment on yourself by becoming an alcoholic? When we look at it in this manner, it is really black and white. It makes sense, yet this type of choice is made all the time.

You can replace the alcoholism with any destructive pattern; the theory is still the same. You either learn from others mistakes or your own, or you are destined to repeat them and to continue the sickness that plagued you. This is where choice is a major part of defining who we are and what we become.

You have the power to make your experience benefit you or destroy you. What you choose to do with your life occurrences is all up to you.

Some of the best counselors and advisors are people who have gone through the same things you have. This is a perfect example of using your situation to benefit yourself and others. You don't have to hide from your experiences. You can look them right in the eye and work with them. Your experiences in life made you what you are. At some point you may even feel gratitude towards them, not necessarily for what was done to you, but for what you were able to walk away with.

Everything in life has a reason. We may not be able to identify that reason while we are going through the situation, but it will come to us when we need it. We collect the pieces of the puzzle and save them until we know just where to place it. It may take days or it may take years, but the connection will always be there, stored away in your memory for safe keeping.

You can also use your experience to benefit yourself and others in a different way besides becoming a counselor or advisor. You can use your emotions, your pain, as fuel. Focus your emotions and put them in to something beautiful. Start painting or drawing. Start writing. Start doing crafts or some type of hobby that is creative. You don't need to be trained to do art. The only thing you need to know how to do is put a piece of paper in front of you and some paints and raise your hands. You don't need to be a trained writer or craftsmen, get the idea completely out of your head. All you need to have is an emotion waiting to come out.

You can even put yourself into music. Sing, dance, or play an instrument. There are so many creative outlets that you can utilize for the pent up energy your emotions bring. What is amazing is that you may even find beauty out of what brought you darkness.

If you feel angry or hurt or just confused, train yourself to channel these emotions to your benefit. You may cry while creating your painting or writing. Let it all out. That is what it is there for. When you take charge of your thoughts and feelings, you begin to realize that no one has control over who you are. What you are doing is taking back what was rightfully yours in the first place, your heart.

You don't have to be crippled by your situation in life. You can make something of yourself and your situation by being willing to look at it from another perspective. It's good to look at your issues, identify them, and feel the emotions that may have been pent up inside of you. Then there is the time when you need to pick yourself up off the ground and free yourself from the control these issues had over you. You can spend years and years reliving your pain, but until you actually are willing to release the emotion, the pain will not subside. Be willing to let go.

Letting go does not mean that the issue was acceptable or right. It just means that you are willing to take what you can from the situation and move on. Don't continue to let it hold you down or be the anchor on your feet. That in itself can be used as an excuse for not getting better. It is your responsibility for standing up, not the person that inflicted your discomfort.

Get out your journal and start a section called 'turning darkness to light.' Come up with some ideas that you could use as a positive outlet for the experiences you have had in life. Don't put any limitations on yourself in this exercise, just allow yourself to write. How do you think your unhealthy experiences could benefit you now? What have you gained from these experiences? When you feel a lot of emotion, what do you do as a healthy form or release?

If you don't have a creative activity or outlet, think about what activities you would be willing to try. Write about it. Make a plan to actually initiate this creativity by going out and getting some basic supplies so that you have them ahead of time. Try dedicating 10-20 minutes a day doing a creative activity. Even if you do this a couple times a week, you may find it quite comforting and even enjoyable.

The excuse, "I'm not creative," is entirely unacceptable. Anyone can be creative; they just need to take the time out to allow their creative nature to come out. You don't have to be a professional artist, writer, or musician to enjoy the creativity that these arts allow. Just do what comes natural to you. Be willing to explore different activities as you may find one fits you more than the other.

Keep writing in your journal about how you feel. It will give you confidence and help you realize that you do own your own thoughts and feelings and you can turn darkness to light.

Exercise #13 Journal Entry Summary

1. Get out your journal and start a section called 'turning darkness to light.' Come up with some ideas that you could use as a positive outlet for the experiences you have had in life. Don't put any limitations on yourself here, just allow yourself to write. How do you think your unhealthy experiences could benefit you now? What have you gained from these experiences? When you feel a lot of emotion, what do you do as a healthy form or release?

2. If you don't have a creative activity or outlet, think about what activities you would be willing to try. Write about it. Make a plan to actually initiate this creativity by going out and getting some basic supplies so that you have them ahead of time. Try dedicating 10-20 minutes a day doing a creative activity.

Exercise 14

Making New Habits

One of the most challenging issues to contend with when you are dealing with unhealthy relationships isn't always the relationship itself, but the aftermath. You can rid yourself of the problem, but the cause still remains. It can be a viscous cycle that no matter how dormant it may be, once you return to the situation, the behavior returns as well.

It's not always easy to recognize its return until you are already involved in another relationship. What's even worse is when you are in an actual healthy relationship and old fears find themselves reemerging. The last thing you want to do is affect your opportunity to have a healthy relationship by spending a lot of time rehashing old issues.

It's perfectly fine to work through your issues with your new partner, but be sure to communicate them first. You have to let them know what you are going through. Be honest about these things when they come up. This will allow you to test out the type of relationship you are in now, based on how they respond to you.

When you tell them about the issue you are dealing with and some of the old baggage you have, look to see if they are patient with you. Are they willing to listen to you? Are they willing to help you work through the issue and perhaps help you identify the solution? Are they understanding and respectful of your past?

If someone cares for you and they want to be with you, they will be open to discussing some of your previous issues. If they are not respectful of your past, you may want to reevaluate whether or not they are respectful of you. Even when we have taken a good look at ourselves and evaluated who we are, our past is still very much a part of who we are. So keep that in mind if you are with someone that may not want to listen about your past experiences.

Sharing your experiences with someone close to you is one thing, reliving them every day is another. If you find that you cannot let go of your issues and you keep obsessing about past experiences to your partner, you need to reevaluate whether or not you really dealt with them. Your partner can't provide you a solution to a personal battle. They might be able to give you insight or a different opinion, but the solution has to come from you. You are the one required to make the action. Personal development is still personal development even when executed within a partnership.

If you experience a severe amount of depression and you see that you cannot function in any type of relationship due to a prior issue, then you may want to seek counsel. You do not have to live in any type of fear or emotional discomfort and be alone. If you feel that your emotional state is severe then you need to address it and seek help for yourself. Again there are always support groups or counseling options that you can look into.

Don't be afraid to ask for help if you need it. Don't let pride stand in the way of your happiness. Getting involved and active in your recovery is the best thing you can do for yourself. So at any point during your self evaluation you feel that you need outside assistance then by all means do what you feel is in your gut.

If you do feel that you are capable of handling your self reflection once again then return to your notebook and look over some of the exercises that we covered. Read over your 'issues' section and see what you wrote down and look at the date that you made your entry. Was there something that you forgot to write about or overlooked?

Sometimes when we start stirring up our memory, new issues emerge that may have slipped our awareness. This emotional purging allows you to sort through your 'garbage' and recycle it for something you can use. It is possible to have some issues linger in the background while you are addressing other issues. Sometimes it takes the right life situation to help us trigger our memory. View this as nature's way of reminding you there is unfinished business inside.

Entering new relationships especially, can trigger our old behaviors and patterns. They might remind us how we used to do something. They might remind us how we used to feel or reacted to certain behaviors in the past. They may even remind us of old habits that we used to repeat.

If you don't realize the old habits emerging then you just might repeat the same situation you worked so hard to be released from. If you haven't had much practice with your new boundaries or perspectives then you might fall right back in line with some of your old roles.

It takes a lot for us to change our behaviors, because just like anything else, our behaviors become habits. Just like you may get a cup of coffee every morning, you may practice 'enabling' or 'controlling' every day. When you do something daily for years and years it becomes so much a part of you. You may be acting or behaving in a certain manner just because you are accustomed to.

Your habits might involve yourself or they might involve your relationships with others. If we want to make a change in the type of relationships we have then we need to make a change in the way we respond to having relationships. We have to look at what we did before, see whether or not is was beneficial to us and the relationship, and if it was not, work on changing the habit.

There are people out there that have a pattern or habit of infidelity. They constantly seek other partners outside of their relationship because they have grown accustomed to this action. They may have everything they really need, a good partner, children even, but they continue to seek that outside fulfillment of another.

Another example might be someone that enters into a relationship and always plays a passive role instead of being assertive. Maybe they are afraid of upsetting the other person, so they would rather be unhappy, then to cause someone else unhappiness. Although this may sound like a noble jester, it is just that, a jester, one that does not assist your well-being or growth.

What happens here is that the person may create a wall around them, essentially isolating themselves and allowing their partner to determine what is right and what is wrong for them instead of speaking up. This can become a very unhealthy habit. The person may struggle to break the habit and consequently stay in the relationship and continue their own unhappiness.

Once you have actually secured a healthy relationship, your habits can actually follow your old footsteps and continue trying to find their place. You may try to use some of your unhealthy behaviors on your healthy partner and find that they are not very compatible with one another. You can at some extent even jeopardize your healthy relationship because of these habits. This is certainly something you want to watch out for.

If your healthy partner has their own boundaries secured, they might make you aware of some of your behaviors and you can work through them. With the right partner, you can learn a new way of loving and caring for someone. You can grow together through the experience of knowing that the life you lived before can still be a part of you without consuming you.

Exercise #14 Journal Entry Summary

1. Write down what repetitive behaviors you have with relationships. Do you find yourself always playing a certain role in a relationship? Or do you have a certain trait that keeps resurfacing?

2. Are you aware of your behaviors when you are doing them or does a partner usually have to bring them to your attention?

3. Do you communicate to your partner about some of your behaviors? Do they know and understand where you are coming from?

Exercise 15

Taking Care of Yourself

When we get involved in a relationship it takes a lot of cooperation and teamwork. You are both responsible for yourselves even though your lives have become one. A healthy relationship can operate like a well-oiled machine. Like any machine, each part requires maintenance or else the whole machine cannot function.

If you are in a relationship, you are part of this machine. You need to maintenance yourself just like you would any other machine that you use, like your car or computer. You have to take time out to focus on yourself. It doesn't take away from the relationship like some may think, instead it adds to the relationship.

When you do things that make you happy, you can share that happiness with the one you love. You can support one another's interests by taking some time out for your own. Sometimes people get overwhelmed when they get involved in a relationship. They may become overly consumed and lose sight of their own responsibilities. As a result they may leave friends and family behind not even realizing their actions.

The truth is, relationships don't always work out. You may go through several until you get to the right one. In the meantime you have to respect the relationships you do have. Those relationships are usually with family first, then maybe close friends. Chances are your family and close friends that act like family, will be around much longer than some of the love relationships you have in your life.

So, part of taking care of yourself while you are trying different relationships also means taking care of the relationships you already have. Keep in touch with people. Don't lose sight of your identity just because a new partner is in your life. Keeping your identity is one personal boundary you want to make a priority. If someone cares about your well being, they will want you to keep involved with people outside of the relationship, and they will want you to keep the identity they were attracted to in the first place.

Relationships aren't about being secluded or isolated. They are about sharing the life that you already have with someone else. This respect for one another, if healthy, should be mutual between both partners.

If you are in an unhealthy relationship, you may become consumed in the partner. Everything in your life will revolve around this one person's responsibilities and livelihood. The further you get involved, the further you lose site and track of yourself. That is why it is important to maintain a balance and boundary for what is your responsibility and what is not your responsibility.

To separate the responsibility between you and your partner, think about some of these statements and then write about them in a section of your journal called, 'taking care of myself.' Are you trying to be responsible for someone's livelihood such as eating, drinking, and sleeping? Are you taking care of their financial obligations such as paying bills, paying for food, or other material items? Are you trying to take care of their personal hygiene like cleaning their house or cars?

These are all basic ideas or concepts that take time away from you and which are not necessarily your responsibility. Now please note there is a difference between being kind to someone and being motherly or fatherly. It's okay to help someone out if you are able to do so, but pay attention to your motives. If you are overly compromising yourself in the process then the gesture becomes more than a gesture. It becomes a responsibility and one that is not your own.

Of course, if you are in a marriage, you do tend to have more responsibility than you would if you were just dating someone. So keep that in mind when you are assessing your responsibilities. Married couples have to share a lot of responsibilities; house maintenance, child care, and paying the bills are just the start.

If you are married and are making an assessment, you may want to ask yourself if you are taking on too many responsibilities. Are you and your partner equally doing house chores, cooking, working, or taking care of financial obligations? Maybe you are taking on too few of responsibilities and letting your spouse do all the work. If this is the case, take a look at ways that you can start to pitch in more.

Even if your partner doesn't complain about doing all the work, don't just sit back and assume they are content with that. Everyone has work to do whether it is paid work or not. Having an extra hand to help out with allows you both more time to spend taking care of yourselves. Not to mention it gives you more time that you can spend together.

If you have been involved in several unhealthy relationships then you may be use to these familiar habits. When you have started the process of working on yourself and your issues, you are headed in the right direction of taking proper care of yourself. Once you have entered a healthy relationship, taking care of yourself is still a priority. In order to continue the health of the relationship, you need to keep pursuing the things you love to do.

If you love to paint or play music, then continue living your life. Work out time for both your relationship and your hobbies. You may even want to see if your partner would like to work with you at times. Or you may just want to set aside alone time for you and your activity. Be honest about who you are and communicate your desires to your partner. If they respect who you are, then they will understand that your talents are a part of you, and they will respect the time that you spend on them.

After being in a relationship for some time, it is possible to become complacent. The initial chase is over and the relationship has reached a level of security. When this occurs, it is very easy to become relaxed with taking care of ourselves as we have the security of a relationship. Partners don't have to 'try' as much as they did before when they were in the 'dating' phase. They might not dress up as often as they did. They may skip the cologne or perfume. They might skip a lot of the little extras that they enjoyed doing prior to their secured commitment. They might quit taking care of themselves like they did before.

If you catch yourself becoming complacent, try spicing things up a little and recapturing the care you used to lend to yourself. Not only will you get your partner's attention, but you will also awaken your own sense of nourishment.

Just because you are in a relationship does not mean that you should take the gift of partnership for granted nor does it mean your self-improvement should step the sidelines. Being comfortable in a relationship is not a bad trait at all. It's great to feel like you can say and do anything with the person you share your life with.

Think about it, when you are involved in a special relationship and living with this person, they see you under many conditions. Your partner sees you when you wake up, when your hair is going every which way. They see you when you are upset or sad. They see you when you are embarrassed or happy.

Maybe you used to exercise before you met your partner. You might have had a daily exercise routine and you looked after your diet and health. Then once you got involved in a relationship, you slowly stopped doing those things. Think about yourself for a moment and then ask yourself what you may have slacked on once you became involved in a relationship.

Was there something you used to do that you enjoyed prior to your relationship? If there was, ask yourself why you stopped doing it? Take a look at what prevents you from starting up some of these old activities or qualities.

Make two columns and write down in the first column what you do right now to take care of yourself. Then in the second column write down what you can do to make improvements on yourself. Do you get enough rest, eat properly, and exercise? Do you take time out for yourself? Are you doing things you enjoy? Are you using all of your talents?

It's important to continue taking care of yourself whether you are in a relationship or not. In fact, this is your life long challenge. If you are actually able to find the balance that you need in your life, then everything else will fall into place. What is even better is that you will notice that as long as the foundation of yourself is strong, nothing else will affect you like it had before. You will be able to bounce back a lot quicker when difficult situations do present themselves.

We must look inside the core of our being and focus on what we need, then what we can give. When you do this you might discover that you are not ready for a relationship right now. Maybe there is more that you need to learn about yourself before you can share it with someone else. Or you may find that you feel you are ready for a commitment and partnership. You won't know until you look inside and do some soul searching.

A lot of times what happens is the opposite occurs. People become involved in a relationship first and then find different aspects of themselves. However you stumble upon who you are doesn't matter, just so you stop to take notes along the way. Sometimes we have to learn about what we want and what we are, by being with people that we wouldn't want to be.

You can really walk away with a more compassionate, but strengthened perspective after getting out of an unhealthy relationship. Hopefully you will take the time out and give yourself a well deserved break to gain focus on where you just came from.

Exercise #15 Journal Entry Summary

1. To separate the responsibility between you and your partner, think about some of these statements and then write about them in a section in your journal called, 'taking care of myself.' Are you trying to be responsible for someone's livelihood such as eating, drinking, and sleeping? Are you taking care of their financial obligations such as paying bills, paying for food, or other material items? Are you trying to take care of their personal hygiene like cleaning their house or cars?

2. If you are married and are making an assessment, you may want to ask yourself if you are taking on too many responsibilities. Are you and your partner equally doing house chores, cooking, working, or taking care of financial obligations? Maybe you are taking on too few of responsibilities and letting your spouse do all the work. If this is the case, take a look at ways that you can start to pitch in more.

3. Think about yourself for a moment and then ask yourself what you may have slacked on once you became involved in a relationship. Was there something you used to do that you enjoyed prior to your relationship? If there was, ask yourself why you stopped doing it? Take a look at what prevents you from starting up some of these old activities or qualities.

4. Make two columns and write down in the first column what you do right now to take care of yourself. Then in the second column write down what you can do to make improvements on yourself. Do you get enough rest, eat properly, and exercise? Do you take time out for yourself? Are you doing things you enjoy? Are you using all of your talents?

Exercise 16

On the Rebound

Instead of taking time out for themselves after a relationship, sometimes the opposite occurs and people jump from one serious relationship to another. This can be beneficial for some and distancing for others. Sometimes the only way people can recover from one relationship is by quickly seeking security with another.

What can happen, though, is that security they think that they are getting is really the same lack of security they had. What happens is they spread the sickness from the previous relationship into the new one. This occurs mainly because the previous issues or baggage did not have time to be dealt with. Instead they were covered over and replaced with a different face.

It is very easy to do this. Sometimes there is a partner out there that gives us strength to leave one relationship. Maybe they allowed you to see something in yourself or in your current relationship that you overlooked. These relationships are gifts in their own right. Granted they might not be serious commitments or last very long, but they can allow people with low self esteem to gain the strength to step out of their current situation.

Some relationships created out of these means turn into life long partnerships and some last only a month or so after the initial unhealthy relationship has terminated. You can view these as catalysts. These relationships usually start as affairs of the heart. They can really be complicated triangles, not one that is recommended, but they occur quite frequently.

An alternative to an affair might be to either end the current relationship or to discuss with your partner your inability to commit to the relationship at this time. The mere concept of having an affair indicates that there is something wrong in your current relationship.

Either there is something seriously missing from the partnership or there is something missing in you alone.

This is easier said than done. If you are feeling unappreciated in the relationship, then your heart might wander to someone that shows you that initial extra attention. You may also be addicted to the fact that you have two people interested in you. It might give you a sense of power or control in a relationship where you feel you have none.

Then there is the confusion state, where you are unsure of what partner to pick. One provides you a sense of security while the other partner is new and you are unsure of the outcome. Meanwhile on the inside what is going on here is that you have created such a situation that you can no longer focus on yourself or your needs. Instead you are focusing on the love triangle before you.

Take a moment to write down in a journal some of your own situations. Take a look at the relationships you had and then think about how they evolved. Were they one right after the other? Did you have an affair and start the second relationship before the first ended?

If you had an affair, be honest with your involvement here. Nobody deserves to be cheated on or lied to because it is unnecessary. No matter how you feel at the time of the occurrence it is not an excuse to mistreat someone. This is where you come in. If you are in a bad situation or an unhealthy relationship then get out of it. Don't just prolong your own agony and create a thrill seeking affair to distract you. All it does is prevent you from facing the facts about your relationship. Whether it is a marriage or dating does not make the action any more valid. If you want honesty in your life that is exactly what you need to give others.

If you are seeking affairs as a form of revenge on a partner that had an affair, you will find that it will not take away the emotion. Your pain will still remain until you discuss it with your partner or release the unhealthy relationship.

If you are the type of person that runs from relationship to relationship with no or little time in between, you have an interesting development going on. Relationships in the first place can provide someone a sense of security. They can make you feel like you have the security of knowing that someone cares for you or loves you. This may not always be a healthy reality, but it is the perception.

This can be derived from a subconscious fear of being alone. The person would rather choose a relationship out of convenience instead of love, *true* love. Instead of waiting for a healthy relationship, this type of person will enter into a functional relationship that is easily maintained and easily created. It might not be exactly what they want, but it is okay for the time being, so they enter into it despite any secret doubts they may have. Instead of having love happen naturally, they feel as though they can learn to love the person they are with.

Instead of falling in love right from the start, they fall in love with the idea of knowing someone will be there when they come home or when they choose to be there. The relationship may actually work for months or years but fizzles out shortly once the freshness of the relationship wears off. If the relationship actually continues, the person will ultimately suffer from their own unhappiness depending on how deeply they have evolved.

Then they might finally end the relationship only to replace another relationship quickly in its place. Instead of taking time to review the previous relationship, they attach themselves to another person available out of convenience. It becomes a cycle, a habit. Therefore the unhappiness in the relationship and in oneself continues.

They also might feel as though they are a failure in relationships because one did not work. So they quickly set out to prove to others that they can acquire another relationship in its place.

The root of the issue can be found in the person themselves. They want stability or a sense of the concept because they lack stability within themselves. So they found a relationship because they think this will solve their problem. In all actuality they needed to pause and reflect and spend time learning more about themselves instead of a new partner.

Then there is the person that quickly gets involved in another relationship to try and replace the loss they feel from the previous relationship. This is the classic case of the rebound relationship. The person finds themselves rehashing old wounds from the other relationship into the new one. They usually find compassionate partners to associate themselves with as they will 'listen' to their issues.

The only problem is that this person has trouble going forward in the current relationship because they are focusing on the past relationship. Sometimes they even keep in contact with the previous partner, never fully letting go, therefore never fully moving on.

You may have experienced one of these situations or none at all. You may have different circumstances entirely. Write down some of the circumstances you experienced. Are there any relationships you felt you rushed into? Are there any relationships that you felt you needed to resolve previous issues? What were they? Can you see how each relationship had prepared you for the next one?

When you are all done with your journal entry, pause for reflection.

Exercise #16 Journal Entry Summary

1. Take a moment to write down in a journal some of your own situations. Take a look at the relationships you had and the think about how they evolved. Were they one right after the other? Did you have an affair and start the second relationship before the first ended?

2. Write down some of the circumstances you experienced. Are there any relationships you felt you rushed into? Are there any relationships that you felt you needed to resolve previous issues? What were they? Can you see how each relationship you had prepared you for the next one?

Exercise 17

Abandon Drama

Let's face it, if you want drama, go see a movie. The screen is a better place for drama then in your own relationship. The difference between your relationship and a movie is that there are real people involved not just characters. If you are that addicted to drama, there are plenty of community theaters you can audition for, but your relationship is certainly not one of them.

Some people can enter a perfectly suitable relationship and then create their own drama without even realizing it. If there is not something wrong, they will find something no matter what the size and blow it into grandiose proportions. The main reason for doing this is they cannot deal with having everything going their way. Something always has to be wrong in order for them to live their life.

As they spend all this time focusing on other people's dramas or their own, they continue to grow further and further away from themselves. As long as they have something negative to focus on, they don't have to focus on who they are. Instead, they focus on outside interferences. They might focus on minute traits of their partner. They might focus on a neighbor's health problems or personal issues. Anything they can do to keep the focus off of them, they will do.

Some people might describe this person as a pessimist or a hypochondriac. However you look at it, they have issues accepting that everything is simply ok. There is no middle ground or sense of balance for them. Things are either very bad or something is wrong.

If the person is involved in a work situation, they can tend to become wrapped up in the different personalities present in the work place. The more people involved, the greater the distraction. This type of person has trouble letting go and trouble accepting any amount of imperfection.

The truth is, they are really looking to be perfect within themselves. If they can't remedy that perfection, they seek others' imperfections to compensate. The cycle continues. So the further away they get from themselves, the more they seek satisfaction in others' faults or illusion of faults.

If you sit down and focus on yourself honestly, you will realize that you don't have time for all the distractions. Taking care of yourself is a full-time job with lots of over-time. You can learn new things about yourself every day if you just take the time to do so.

The best way to determine if you are giving yourself the right amount of attention is to look at where your attention is actually going. Get out your journal and ask yourself what responsibilities you focus on every day. Is there anything that takes up your time or overly consumes you? Do you find yourself focusing on others issues or faults more then your own?

When someone asks you how you are feeling, do you always answer negatively or are there days where you can say that you are simply fine? Write down about what drama you have in your life. Then look at how much of the drama is initiated by you. If the drama does not stem from you personally, look at where it does come from. Does it come from situations or people you chose to involve yourself with?

If you want to take ownership of your life, you have to be willing to accept that you participate in the choices that are made. Nobody forces you to be involved in certain relationships or situations. Some situations are not in our control, but a lot are. You can choose who you involve yourself with and what type of situations you attract. Writing in your journal will allow you to identify and evaluate the dramas created in your life. Keep check on yourself and perform this exercise any time you are feeling overwhelmed with your life. This will help you prioritize your feelings and emotional responsibilities.

Exercise #17 Journal Entry Summary

1. Get out your journal and ask yourself what responsibilities you focus on every day. Is there anything that takes up your time or overly consumes you? Do you find yourself focusing on others issues or faults more then your own?

2. When someone asks you how you are feeling, do you always answer negatively or are there days where you can say that you are simply fine? Write down about what drama you have in your life. Then look at how much of the drama is initiated by you. If the drama does not stem from you personally, look at where it does come from. Does it come from situations or people you chose to involve yourself with?

Exercise 18

Quality of Life Assessment

One of the keys to obtaining a better life or living arrangement is to assess the quality of relationships that you surround yourself with. Do you surround yourself with loving relationships or unhealthy relationships? For someone that has a pattern or history with unhealthy relationships, the difference between the two may be difficult to decipher.

Healthy relationships are relationships that add to our well being, not subtract. They bring out the best of us by being supportive of our goals and our inner selves. Unhealthy relationships often cause us stress and subtract from our well being, often leaving us feeling depleted of energy.

We went over several exercises that allowed you to assess the types of relationships you have had from past to present. Now we need to assess your over all quality of life. Our relationships and the type of people we surround ourselves with on a daily basis affect and influence our own perspectives. If you are constantly surrounded by negative minded people then in turn your outlook will be affected towards negativity. Or you may simply find it a struggle to maintain a positive outlook when you keep coming in contact with negative people.

All of these scenarios contribute to our overall well being so much, especially if you have not taken the time to strengthen your own ideas and perspectives. That is why it is essential to establish a firm sense of self no matter what type of lifestyle you have. When we develop a strong foundation, we are able to be in almost any type of environment, either positive or negative, and see our way through. When you are armed with integrity and self awareness, others' energy, whether positive or negative, turns from influences to just opinions.

Did you ever notice how being around some people just makes you feel good? No matter what is going on in your life when you are around these people, something just always makes you feel okay. That is because these people give off a positive energy that is contagious. Just imagine what it would be like to be with someone positive, either in friendship or a love relationship. You would feel good most of the time. You would be able to get along with one another because you both have a healthy outlook on life and yourself. What a powerful and igniting combination.

Becoming involved in a healthy relationship is one thing, surrounding yourself with positive people in general is another. In actuality, once you start to weed through your friends or associates you will discover just how many of those relationships are based on false pretenses. You will discover that those people you thought would support you, actually were only there for the moment when it was right for them.

We can't avoid negativity. It is around us on a daily basis. You may find it at the grocery store or in your car on the roadways. You may find it in your work environment or even in your family. It is unavoidable, but you can take steps to minimize your involvement and interaction.

One of the first ways of protecting yourself is through knowledge. The more you can comprehend about your own thoughts and feelings, the better. Knowing yourself and establishing that firm foundation, starts by assessing who you are and what you believe in. This way you take on the role of becoming a leader instead of being easily swayed to believe in someone else's beliefs. There are people out there that are predators for this type of personality. Some unfortunately are in great positions of authority and others are just your average person.

If you define who you are, you create a concrete base for that of which you can measure all other influences. Your ideas and thoughts may change as time progresses, but at least it is you making the choice to change, not someone else. A true person of power need not persuade anyone. They merely need stand as an example.

A lot of people think they know themselves and perhaps they do. Then there are other people out there that have walked around inside the same body for years, even decades and they don't know who they are or what they stand for. Sometimes people just forget and need reminded. It is easy to do when you get sidetracked with work, friends, or even family. Keeping yourself busy in life doesn't mean that you necessarily know everything about yourself. In fact, the opposite could be true.

The more we get sidetracked with being social or overworking ourselves, the further away we can get from the introspective moments that allow us to identify our true nature and thoughts. It's easy to go out every night or go to work every day. That is easy. It's challenging when you spend that same amount of time with yourself. If you don't agree, try it and make note of your results.

The ironic thing is people that may have the most friends or associates in their lives, may actually be the loneliest of people. If they don't have a firm foundation of self established, they can get easily get lost in socializations.. It's easy to get lost in the environment around you. It's easy to absorb your surroundings instead of observing them. We might get so caught up in the function that we forget about the process.

It is important that we take time to assess who we are and where we want to go. Then we are able to assess the people around us and see whether or not they fit into our overall well-being. Start writing in your journal, label this exercise, 'who I am,' or whatever you prefer. Begin by describing yourself as you would a reporter doing an interview. The only difference here is we are going to really break it down into very trivial questions, questions you would assume you know off the top of your head. Start by asking yourself some of the questions listed below.

Who I Am Assessment

1. What is your favorite color?
2. What is your favorite food?

3. Where would you love to visit?
4. Where would you love to live?
5. What are your hobbies?
6. What would you like to accomplish in your life?
7. What are some of your immediate goals?
8. What are some of your goals for the future?
9. What is most valuable to you in your life?
10. If you could do anything in the world what would it be?

For people that have been involved with unhealthy relationships, you would be amazed at how difficult these basic questions can be to answer. Especially if you have spent time focusing on someone else instead of yourself. Sure you might know what your partner's favorite color or goals are, but did you recall your own? It just goes to show how lost we can become in someone else's world, that we can forget our own small details.

So begin by writing down these questions and answering them. Make notes or star the questions that you had to think about just so you can see where you were at with your assessment. If you had zero stars then congratulations you know yourself rather well. If you had a few stars checked then you are on your way to getting a better hold of who you are. If you had over five stars then you need to spend some more time writing in your journal about some of your life goals and outlooks.

Even taking a half hour out of your day to work on organizing your goals could prove to be quite beneficial for anyone. Maybe even spend every other day or so taking some quiet time out for yourself to focus on meditations. Taking time out to reflect is extremely crucial. It allows you to organize your thoughts. It allows you to collect yourself from the situations you are asked to face daily.

If we don't take this time to cleanse ourselves of our daily encounters, then they build up and begin to create clutter in our minds. The only reasonable way to resolve ourselves from this distress is to be willing to let it all out from time to time. You don't have to spend hours in meditation every day; however, you may find yourself seeking refuge in its comfort.

Meditation can be your only time for tranquility in the busy world we live in. So savor it, and replace your unhealthy habits with healthy ones. Meditation is rather simple and can be done anywhere you feel most comfortable. Just try to make sure you are not going to be bothered by phone calls, excessive noise, or other disturbances, such as people.

You want to be with yourself and yourself alone. If you live with a spouse, family, or roommate, tell them you are not to be bothered for a set amount of time. It's important that once you actually get your train of thought or focus, that you have uninterrupted time to explore it.

You don't have to do this all the time, but it certainly is a safe haven for you to become recluse. After your meditation sessions, put some notes in your journal just to kind of recapture some of the thoughts that came to you. Keep doing your meditation as often as you feel necessary. This will help you gain your focus and work on creating a healthier mental space.

Another way of removing some of the negativity from your life, besides getting to know yourself, would be to actually spend time with yourself. Sure you might think that getting ready for work or taking a shower is spending time, but they are really just a matter of function and necessity. The time we are referring to is personal time.

Meditation is just a start as it makes you sit down for a moment in stillness. Spending time with yourself is when you sit down to appreciate things you enjoy doing. Maybe you like to work in a garden or take care of your lawn. You might like to paint or draw. Maybe you like putting model cars together or even coloring in a kids coloring book (even if you don't have kids). Doing activities by yourself that you enjoy, means spending quality time with yourself.

You don't always have to be focusing on your issues or goals. You can also find the time to have fun with yourself. After all, if you can't enjoy your own company, how could you expect someone else to? You don't always have to do these fun things alone, but to start out it is recommended.

A lot of times people don't even think about setting time aside to be by themselves. Especially if you are coming from an unhealthy relationship, where you are accustomed to being with someone all the time, you won't know what to do with the mental and physical space. That's why we have to practice each week or if possible each day.

Unhealthy relationships take so much away from our lives without us even knowing. Years may pass and along with those years, we slowly lose ourselves in the process of trying to please or battle with the partner. There is a much more efficient way of using our time and energy. There is a much more loving way to live.

If you don't have a hobby or know what you like to do, look over the list you just created. If you were unable to answer some of those questions or got stumped, it is time to discover what you enjoy. Getting out of an unhealthy relationship and removing some of the unhealthy obstacles in your life can be an amazing breath of fresh air. You may have more time to yourself, but that is probably because you need it. The universe has a great way of giving us space at exactly the right moment in our lives, even when we disagree with the timing.

Be willing to make the sacrifice. If you have to separate yourself from a socially busy lifestyle, then do it. You may feel like you might be missing out on something, but you are not. You are gaining something more than you could ever gain from someone else; yourself. So take pride in knowing that any type of sacrifice you make right now, you will be rewarded for your time and effort.

If we want to get the most we can out of ourselves, we have to be willing to put fourth a certain amount of dedication. We have to be willing to set time aside from outside temptations. View this as a challenge for you to decipher what is a priority and what really is not a priority. Put as much time into yourself as you would any other devoted relationship.

We forget that we have a relationship going with ourselves. Just like a relationship with another person, we have to nurture ourselves, spend quality time, and show ourselves just how loved we really are. If you have mistreated yourself, then you owe yourself an apology. If you have mistreated your body then you need to tell yourself that you are sorry. If you have done anything to jeopardize your health then you need to make amends with yourself, just like you would do for anyone else.

It is about self respect. If you don't have self respect then you probably don't have self control, because the two go hand in hand. It is time to regain that which is rightfully yours; your life. Embrace it and make it your own.

For our next journal exercise, make a section called, 'Self Care Assessment', answer the following set of questions:

1. Have you been paying attention to your health?
2. Are you eating properly for your body size?
3. Are you overweight or underweight?
4. Are you exercising?
5. What type of exercise do you do and how often?
6. Are you happy with your current work situation?
7. Are you doing something you enjoy?
8. How often are you drinking alcohol, taking unprescribed drugs, or illegal substances?
9. When you are upset or emotionally distraught how do you deal with it? What do you do?
10. Now that you have answered all the questions above, what could you do to take better care of yourself that you are not doing right now?

This exercise helps you become aware of how well you take care of yourself. Nobody is going to judge you except for yourself. Only you see the answers before you. You are not in a doctor or counselor's office having to confess your faults in front of another person. It is just you and your journal. Tell the truth to yourself first and then if you feel comfortable you can share your new findings with someone else you trust, a close friend, partner, or counselor. Or you can keep this information to yourself, it doesn't matter.

What does matter is that you learn from your assessment. Take the information you found out about yourself and use it wisely. Getting better in our life, starts by us making a healthy plan, and putting it into action.

Exercise #18 Journal Entry Summary

A. Make a section in your journal called, 'Who I Am Assessment' and answer the following questions.

1. What is your favorite color?
2. What is your favorite food?
3. Where would you love to visit?
4. Where would you love to live?
5. What are your hobbies?
6. What would you like to accomplish in your life?
7. What are some of your immediate goals?
8. What are some of your goals for the future?
9. What is most valuable to you in your life?
10. If you could do anything in the world what would it be?

B. For our next journal exercise, make a section called, 'Self Care Assessment', answer the following set of questions:

1. Have you been paying attention to your health?

2. Are you eating properly for your body size?

3. Are you overweight or underweight?

4. Are you exercising?

5. What type of exercise do you do and how often?

6. Are you happy with your current work situation?

7. Are you doing something you enjoy?

8. How often are you drinking alcohol, taking unprescribed drugs, or illegal substances?

9. When you are upset or emotionally distraught how do you deal with it? What do you do?

10. Now that you have answered all the questions above, what could you do to take better care of yourself that you are not doing right now?

Exercise 19

A Healthy Self Image

If you have actually followed through and made it up to this exercise you deserve to give yourself a big pat on the back. You have performed something that few people would have dared to do, you looked at yourself. You should be proud of what you have uncovered.

You learned how to identify your behavior and others behavior and then determine what was healthy and unhealthy. You learned how to look for patterns in your life and discover why you were doing some of the things you were doing. Then you learned how to deal with your past issues and bring them into the forefront. You learned how to forgive yourself and how to recover from your grief.

You are bound to feel emotionally exhausted from all the personal excavating you have done. You picked through every crevice of emotion you had and took a good, hard look at your life for how it truly is. Now it is time to work on repairing your self image. Your self image can be how you view or look at yourself. Your self image is basically the microscope you hold yourself under every time you look in the mirror.

There might be certain things you don't like about yourself. Then there may be certain features or traits that you fully appreciate. What we are going to work on is not so much emphasizing the line between the two, but the acceptance of them both. We achieve self love through accepting ourselves as is, instead of as we think we should be.

Acceptance does not mean that we stop caring for ourselves or that we stop advancing. As long as you are taking care of yourself and making progress then the results in your self esteem should be quite evident. If you know that you are at least putting in some effort instead of doing nothing at all, you will feel some sense of accomplishment.

There are basic things you can do daily to improve your self image. You may overlook them sometimes, but they are important tiny steps to feeling better about yourself. Some of these questions may sound redundant, but you would be amazed how many people can forget to tend to themselves after being involved in unhealthy relationships or environments.

Personal Maintenance Assessment:
1. Do you have good dental hygiene?
2. Do you shower and bathe yourself?
3. Are you getting outside to get fresh air?
4. Do you put time and effort into what you wear?
5. Are you getting enough sleep?
6. Are you drinking enough water?
7. Is your personal living space clean or dirty?
8. Are you organized?
9. Are you doing your laundry frequently?
10. Are you standing up straight?

All of these questions may seem so basic, but do not overlook how important they are. There could be one tiny little thing out of place with your appearance or features that throw you off.

For example, maybe you don't want to attract attention from people, so you dress down all the time. This is very common. It's not that the person doesn't want to look good, but perhaps they are nervous about attracting unwanted attention from the opposite or same sex, depending on their preference.

Or maybe someone doesn't like their teeth, so they are afraid to smile or to even talk. Someone may be paranoid about how their face appears so they try to cover it with their hair. All these scenarios are signals that let you know that your confidence is suffering and as a result you are suffering too.

No matter what size you are, no matter how you feel you may look, look your best regardless. Take what you have and make the most of it. For every feature you don't like, work with the features you do like. This is what makes you special. This is what makes you... you.

You want to learn how to take better care of yourself so begin with the basics. Take simple steps towards your self improvement. It doesn't matter if you commit to just getting up and getting dressed every day. If it is something you haven't done for a while due to neglect, then do it. If it means waking up and washing your face or brushing your hair, no matter how small it is, do it.

By making small commitments we can then work on making large commitments. You will be surprised at how big small improvements really are. In fact, you may even start to like how you feel and want to actually do more.

Making healthy choices in our lives depends on how well we take care of ourselves. If we are not healthy then it's hard to make healthy decisions. Taking care of yourself is the foundation from which your life stems.

Make two columns in a separate section in your notebook. You can title this section 'Things I do for me.' One column should be labeled unhealthy and the other healthy. Start by writing down the habits you perform daily that are healthy for you. How do you take care of yourself? What do you do for yourself that makes you feel good about who you are? Just to clarify, we are not talking about what you do for others. We are talking about you, that is where our focus is right now.

When you are done with that column, move on to your 'unhealthy' column and start writing down the things that you do in your life that are unhealthy for you. Once you have completed that section, read over what you wrote thoroughly. Does one column have more than the other? Which one? This will help you see where your balance is with yourself.

This evaluation will allow you to see how well you take care of yourself based on what you have listed in your 'healthy' column. A lot of times people might associate taking care of themselves with conceit and this is not the case. Conceit is about the attitude you convey about yourself. Conceit is about thinking you are better than someone else. Taking care of yourself is about being better than what you were yesterday. There is a difference.

Don't be afraid to be the best you can be daily. Don't focus so much on what others expect of you, but focus more on what you expect from yourself. Do what makes you feel good as long as it is healthy for you.

Take out your journal again and make another section called, 'Taking Care of Myself.' Start listing the things that you can do daily to take better care of yourself. Start out by writing about both short and long term goals for your health and self improvement. Then decide which goals you can get started on right away.

Make a commitment to take care of yourself and work towards your goals daily. For some, this might mean getting dressed every day. For others, this might mean committing to an exercise routine daily. Take whatever steps you think you are capable of handling. Be realistic with yourself.

You don't want to become overwhelmed. What you are looking for here is longevity. You want to create a healthy habit that will last longer than a week. If you can, work on these goals five times a week. In the case of exercise, use your own discretion or contact a physician to negotiate a healthy routine based on your current body type and structure.

You have focused on your commitment to other people and now it is time to focus on your relationship with yourself. Start out small, pick one or two goals you want to commit to. Write a note to yourself and hang it some place where you will see it frequently; a refrigerator door, your bathroom mirror, or your coffee/tea maker. After you keep practicing, soon your goals and new healthy habits will become a part of your daily routine. Eventually you won't even have to think anymore about your commitment to yourself, you will do it naturally.

Exercise #19 Journal Entry Summary

1. Make two columns in a separate section in your notebook. You can title this section 'Things I do for me.' One column should be labeled unhealthy and the other healthy. Start by writing down the habits you perform daily that are healthy for you. How do you take care of yourself? What do you do for yourself that makes you feel good about who you are?

2. When you are done with that column, move on to your 'unhealthy' column and start writing down the things that you do in your life that are unhealthy for you. Once you have completed that section, read over what you wrote thoroughly. Does one column have more than the other? Which one?

3. Make another section called, 'Taking Care of Myself.' Start listing the things that you can do daily to take better care of yourself. Start out by writing about both short and long term goals for your health and self improvement. Then decide which goals you can get started on right away.

4. Start out small, pick one or two goals you want to commit to. Write a note to yourself and hang it some place where you will see it frequently; a refrigerator door, your bathroom mirror, or your coffee/tea maker.

Exercise 20

Growth Assessment

You have made it through the entire book. For some of you, you may have read the book first before completing the exercises and that is purely acceptable. Others may have chosen to read a chapter and work the exercises as they go. Whatever worked for you is fine. The important thing is that you made the step to start and begin a change in yourself. You showed up and that is what is necessary if you expect growth.

When you first started writing in your journal you were asked to date your journal entries and exercises. This was so when you completed the book you could go back and compare who you were when you started, with who you are right now.

Start by turning to your Relationship Assessment sheet that we had you create in Exercise #1.

Notice the date on the assessment. Read over everything again. Do you still feel the same about what you wrote? Or did your perceptions change after you performed further evaluations of yourself through this book?

If there is a relationship that you think you wrote about in the beginning that your perspective changed, circle it with a different color marker or pen. This will allow you to easily pick them out when we need to go back to them.

Also pay close attention the column where you were asked to place 'your role' in the relationship. How do you feel now about that role? Did it change or stay the same? What relationship really stands out now as having a big influence on you?

Write your discoveries down in a section called 'Growth Assessment,' and be sure to date the entry. Discuss what information you feel changed as you went through the other exercises? Did you make any new discoveries about yourself and your involvement? Did your roles change or stay the same?

You may have written down several answers at the time of your assessment that you feel differently about now. So write down what has changed for you. Were there relationships you thought were healthy, but were not? Make note of what made you change your mind. This will allow you to see where you may have had common misperceptions.

Sometimes all you need is a reminder to trigger your memory, something to help you recall situations in your life that may have affected you deeply.

In order to keep yourself in check with your boundaries and beliefs, go back and review your personal boundaries section. You can do this at any time that you have doubts with relationships that you are involved with. Your journal is the black and white of your life. It should honestly tell you about some of the commitments you have made to yourself.

If you completed all the exercises up till now, you have established a strong foundation. You know what you want in a partner. You know what you consider to be healthy and what you feel is unhealthy. You should have an idea of the commitment you set up for yourself.

You should also have an idea of the traits you need to work on with yourself. You should know your strengths and your weaknesses based on the self image assessments you did. Knowing what to change is only part of the solution, working towards correcting your behavior and bettering yourself is the other half.

Make a maintenance plan for yourself. Read over all the exercises that you worked on and make a plan to carry out some of your objectives. Title this entry 'Objectives.' Write about what you learned collectively about yourself and the people you have involved yourself with. Then write about what changes you plan on making in your life. What do you feel confident about now? What do you still have doubts about? Is there a certain aspect of your life that you feel needs extra attention?

When you are counseling and exploring yourself, you have to give yourself the same level of commitment that you would give to any other counseling professional. If you made an appointment with someone, you would hopefully show up. So when you set time aside for yourself, don't back out of it. Respect your own time just as you would someone else's.

As you grow and change, so will your responses to the exercises we performed. So if you feel you need to reevaluate yourself again, simply redo your exercises. You can even develop your own personal assessment too. Make your self improvement a continual process. You don't have to assess your life constantly, but it is good to perform maintenance from time to time. Not to mention it is important to remember where you came from.

A life explored on the inside is a life well lived on the outside. Continue to be patient and know that the best healthy relationship you could ever have is with yourself. This is the core from which all other relationships stem. Make it a priority.

Exercise #20 Journal Entry Summary

1. Create a section in your journal called 'Growth Assessment.' Start by turning to your Relationship Assessment sheet that we had you create in Exercise #1. Notice the date on the assessment. Read over everything again. Do you still feel the same about what you wrote? Or did your perceptions change after you performed further evaluations of yourself through this book?

If there is a relationship that you think you wrote about in the beginning that your perspective changed, circle it with a different color marker or pen. This will allow you to easily pick them out when we need to go back to them.

2. Pay close attention the column where you were asked to place 'your role' in the relationship. How do you feel now about that role? Did it change or stay the same? What relationship really stands out now as having a big influence on you?

3. Make a maintenance plan for yourself. Read over all the exercises that you worked on and make a plan to carry out some of your objectives. Title this entry 'Objectives.' Write about what you learned collectively about yourself and the people you have involved yourself with. Then write about what changes you plan on making in your life. What do you feel confident about now? What do you still have doubts about? Is there a certain aspect of your life that you feel needs extra attention?

[1] Alcohol Health & Research World

[2] Washington Post
http://www.washingtonpost.com/wp-dyn/articles/A29751-2004Dec2.html

[3] FDA Calls for Warnings on 10 Antidepressant Drugs:
Celexa, Effexor, Lexapro, Luvox, Paxil, Prozac, Remeron, Serzone, Wellbutrin, Zoloft
http://hbcprotocols.com/antidepressant.html

[4] The National Crime Victimization Survey (NCVS)
http://www.ojp.usdoj.gov/bjs/cvict.htm

[5] *Rape in America: A Report to the Nation*

[6] "Divorce statistics collection: Summary of findings so far," Americans for Divorce Reform, at:
http://www.divorcereform.org/results.html